THE COUNTRY DIARY
OF A SUFFOLK
NATURALIST

by
Rob Macklin

In memory of

Andrew Robin Pow

*who loved nature, loved life
and brightened each day with his
sunny disposition*

ISBN 978-0-9556604-0-5

Author: Rob Macklin
Design: John Grant

First published 2007

Rob Macklin,
River Hundred, Aldeburgh Road,
Aldringham, Suffolk IP16 4QP

Printed by
Healeys Printers Ltd
Unit 10, The Sterling Complex,
Farthing Road, Ipswich, Suffolk IP1 5AP

Front cover: The Hundred River

Contents

Acknowledgements

I am particularly indebted to Stuart Elsom and Mark Breaks for the majority of the bird photographs, but also to the following photographic contributors; John Archibald, Kathy Archibald, Ian Barthorpe, Peter Beesley, Nicola Breaks, Graham Catley, John Davies, Robin Harvey, Jim Law, Neil Loverock, Terry McGeever, Mike Page, Allen Pocock, Steve Robinson, Adam Rowlands, Richard Thomas and Steve Valentine.

Special thanks to John Grant and his wife Sheena for designing the book and proof reading and to Mike Gaydon at Healeys for putting it all together. Finally, this book would not have been possible without the help and support of my wife Kathy.

Bibliography

1. *Wild Food*, Roger Phillips, Peerage Books 1988.
2. *Mushrooms*, Roger Phillips, Pan Books 1981.
3. *Flora Britannica*, Richard Mabey, Sinclair-Stevenson 1996.
4. *The Springs of Joy*, Tasha Tudor, Rand McNally & Co 1979.
5. *The Country Diary of an Edwardian Lady*, Edith Holden, Webb & Bower 1978.
6. *St. Peter's Church, Thorington*, Judith Middleton Stewart

Foreword

This book was inspired by Edith Holden's "The Country Diary of an Edwardian Lady" which recorded natural history events in the year 1906. The book detailed her observations surrounding her home in Warwickshire and on her travels throughout England and Scotland.

The world has changed since that time but it seemed appropriate to keep a country diary on the 100th anniversary of that remarkable book. This book will focus on my observations on the Suffolk coast, particularly around the Royal Society for the Protection of Birds' nature reserve at North Warren, near Aldeburgh. It also includes observations on my travels to California, Hungary, Exmoor and Somerset.

The North Warren nature reserve is the second oldest in the RSPB's portfolio, with the initial purchase of land taking place here in 1938. Further parcels were added in 1972, 1990 and 1995 and the area of land now under conservation management totals 442 hectares. The reserve boasts a complex network of habitats including reedbeds, grazing marshes, wild open heath, vegetated shingle, diverse woodland and associated scrub.

Wildlife abounds here!

There is no season such
delight can bring
as summer, autumn,
winter and the spring.

William Browne

In winter the grazing marshes are allowed to flood by closing the main sluices and this attracts a truly remarkable array of wildfowl and wading birds. Wild geese arrive from the far north from November onwards, particularly white-fronted geese and occasionally tundra bean geese. Several thousand wigeon and teal are joined by smaller numbers of gadwall, shoveler and pintail. When the River Alde reaches high tide at Slaughden thousands of dunlin and lapwings use the marshes as a safe roost. In spring, breeding redshanks and lapwings bring the marshes to life with their joyous calls and tumbling, aerobatic displays, while the seven miles of reedy dykes attract a wide range of gaudy dragonflies. Skylarks breed in amazing numbers and must be as abundant here as anywhere in England.

The reedbeds resound to the sound of booming male bitterns from early spring and in 2006 three pairs nested here. This small reedbed holds the highest density of breeding bitterns in England, although outnumbered by nine booming males at nearby Minsmere. Marsh harriers breed every year and their breathtaking skydiving display flights are a sight to behold in spring. A host of smaller birds inhabit the dense reedbeds, particularly reed buntings, exotic bearded tits, reed warblers and sedge warblers plus the highly vocal, but rarely seen, Cetti's warblers. Otters hunt for eels and other fish along the Hundred river, while water voles burrow into the reedbed banks.

Hawthorn in full bloom   *Photo:* Rob Macklin

From early February the open heath rings with the beautiful fluty notes of singing woodlarks; this smaller and scarcer relative of the skylark has staged a comeback in recent years and now thrives at the reserve. Moving into April and the first warblers arrive from Africa – chiffchaffs and blackcaps – while the first sand martins and swallows search hungrily for any available insects. Flowering blackthorn provides a vital nectar source for early emerging butterflies such as commas and peacocks. As spring moves into early summer, nightingales sing from thickets of hawthorn, blackthorn and bramble. More warblers soon arrive in the shape of hundreds of whitethroats, lesser whitethroats and garden warblers. Swifts scream overhead and cuckoos begin to call, although this harbinger of spring has become much less common in recent years.

In the heat of mid-summer, glow-worms thrive on the heath while nightjars *"churr"* magically at dawn and dusk. Dartford warblers and stonechats raise broods in the dense thickets of heather and gorse. Butterflies and dragonflies abound along the paths across the reserve and summer flowers bring a riot of colour. Orchids appear in the rough grassland while the fen blooms with the yellows, whites and pinks of yellow rattle, meadowsweet, ragged robin and purple loosestrife. The thought of autumn is never far away as wading birds such as greenshanks and black-tailed godwits return from their northern breeding grounds.

Autumn brings a blaze of reds and yellows and our summer birds begin to make their way south. Unusual migrants often occur on the coast and this year a very rare red-flanked bluetail put in an appearance at Thorpeness Common, attracting a horde of birdwatchers! A wide range of fungi erupts from the pastures and the woodland floor, some edible such as horse mushrooms, but some best avoided, such as the spectacular fly agaric.

Yellow rattle adds a touch of colour in the fen   *Photo:* Rob Macklin

And so to the end of the year; cattle leave the marshes for their winter quarters, the remaining grass on the marshes is cut and wildfowl begin to trickle in. The sluices are closed once more from mid-November and the annual cycle begins again.

The first month of the year in the Roman calendar was named after the god Janus. Janus had two faces which allowed him to look backwards into the old year and forward into the new year at the same time. He was the "spirit of the opening".

The Anglo-Saxons called the month "Wolf Monath" as the first wolves came into the villages in winter in search of food.

Birch woods at River Hundred in winter   *Photo:* Rob Macklin

1st

The new year dawned with grey skies and some remnants of snow on the boardwalk through the fen. In the wood I found the remains of a redwing which had probably been taken by a sparrowhawk. The mild conditions have tempted great, blue and coal tits into song; two robins were singing in the churchyard at Aldringham. I flushed a woodcock from bracken in Church Wood.

January
2nd

A small group of redwings were feeding in the birches at River Hundred while a flock of 15 siskins and a single brambling preferred the nearby alders. Small groups of long-tailed tits and goldcrests tumbled together from tree to tree.

Redwing at River Hundred   *Photo:* Graham P. Catley, Nyctea.co.uk

Male bearded tit on reeds   *Photo:* Mark Breaks

Walked along the south bank of the reedbed in the afternoon; three female marsh harriers drifted in and out of the pale yellow reeds, including one with black and white upperwings and back! A male bearded tit feeding avidly on reed seedheads ignored my intrusion into his world.

On the way home a muntjac darted away through the undergrowth with a characteristic flash of its white undertail. The Reeves muntjac or barking deer is a native of South-East Asia and was introduced into Britain at Woburn Abbey in the nineteenth century. The most significant release of this species was from Whipsnade Zoo in 1921 and our current feral population probably stems from this release!

Male muntjac at River Hundred   *Photo:* Rob Macklin

4th

A s the sun came out later in the morning the first woodlark of the year was singing over the heath at Snape Warren. Checked out the marshes at North Warren in the afternoon and as well as the usual greylags and Canadas, 48 barnacle geese were on the Sluice Marsh with 210 white-fronted geese spread out over the rest of North Marsh. Winter rabbit survival looked good on the heath with at least 160 adults seen above ground in just two fields. Very little colour except for the stunning yellow of the gorse flowers. Moles have invaded the garden at River Hundred.

Winter-flowering gorse   *Photo:* Rob Macklin

January
9th

Sunny, bright and a little milder with an easterly breeze. Sunrise over Aldeburgh beach was a sight to behold. Walked up to Aldringham Church then on to the Walks. Lots of magpies around and the outdoor pig units had attracted some 1,000 assorted gulls and over 250 carrion crows; 200 linnets and a few meadow pipits were foraging on an area of fallow ground. I came across red deer tracks on the north edge of Square Covert then flushed a delightful group of eight woodlarks from a weedy stubble field. A great-spotted woodpecker flew across the open ground on the Walks before finding the safety of cover in Corporal's Belt. On the way home I counted one male and at least six female marsh harriers coming into their reedbed roost. I could hear the yelping calls of white-fronted geese on North Marsh and counted over 170 birds.

Sunrise over the North Sea   *Photo:* John Davies

Male great-spotted woodpecker   *Photo:* Stuart Elsom

White-fronted geese in flight   *Photo:* Stuart Elsom

The whole month has been cloudy, grey and dull but today a breezy north-westerly wind blew the clouds away. Walked along the old railway track at North Warren and the marshes looked superb with shallow flooding attracting thousands of wildfowl, particularly wigeon and teal. The white-fronted goose flock numbered some 334 birds, the highest count of the winter so far.

5

Large numbers of greylags were mixed in with their wilder cousins and I also managed to pick out six tundra bean geese – these marshes have been hosting bean geese for well over 100 years. In years gone by farmers used to employ local lads to scare these grey geese from the crops in Suffolk!

The lapwing roost reached over 1,900 birds; most of these will be visitors from northern Europe, drawn south by our relatively balmy winter conditions.

Two female marsh harriers were gliding back and forth over the marshes continually putting the lapwings, wigeon and teal to flight, providing a spectacular display! The harriers themselves were being harassed by several carrion crows which soon persuaded them to retreat to the comparative safety of the reedbed. Clouds of reed seed drifted in the wind across the reedbed creating an ethereal cloak in the fading evening light.

28th

North Warren reedbed in winter   *Photo:* Rob Macklin

Sunny and cold all day with a brisk north-easterly wind blowing in off the sea. Marsh tits were calling by the edge of the reedbed and at River Hundred. Two female marsh harriers circled over the marshes and reedbed. Very quiet on the marshes and no wild geese to be seen!

February was introduced into the Roman calendar by Numa Pompilous when the calendar was extended to twelve months. The word "February" comes from "februa" which means cleansing or purification, reflecting the rituals undertaken before spring.

The Anglo-Saxons called February "Sol Monath (cake month)" because cakes were offered to the gods. It was also known to the Saxons as "sprout-kale" from the sprouting of cabbage or kale. The Romans and Celts regarded February as the start of spring.

Snow bunting foraging on beach   *Photo:* Stuart Elsom

February

2nd

Candlemas Day

If Candlemas Day be fair and bright,
Winter will have another fight.
If Candlemas Day brings cloud and rain,
Winter won't come again.

Grey, overcast and extremely mild, tempting one to wonder if winter could be over! Sixty snow buntings were searching for fallen seeds amongst the remains of the vegetation on the beach. Milder winters have led to a decrease of this "harbinger of winter" on the Suffolk coast but it can still be found occasionally on our beaches.

6th

Grey and dull today as it has been for the past several days and still cold with temperatures no more than 7°C. Occasional short bursts of song from great, blue and coal tits. Put a woodcock up from dead bracken in the birch woods. This most secretive of species lives and breeds mainly in woodland and in winter its numbers are greatly swelled by immigrants from northern Europe. They feed actively under cover of darkness, especially in the winter months, before returning at dawn to spend the day in dense cover.

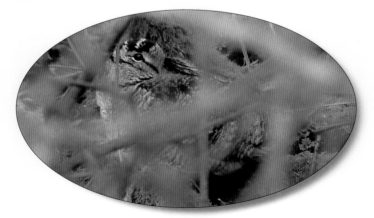

Woodcock hiding in bracken   *Photo:* Allen Pocock

February
8th

A welcome change in the weather brought sunny, clear skies and a cold wind from the north. One or two daffodils now poking through the soil hinted at the new life to come.

Snowdrops at Snape Church made an awesome sight *Photo:* Rob Macklin

9

Snowdrops poking through leaf litter   *Photo:* Rob Macklin

10th

An overnight snow shower was not deep enough to smother the first signs of spring. Drifts of snowdrops in full flower at Snape Church made an awesome sight and I saw my first flowering dandelion at Blackheath Corner.

A male pheasant was enjoying a dust bath in Church Wood at Aldringham and a woodcock got up and flashed away through the trees.

Marsh harriers are a constant feature throughout the year at North Warren and the reedbed is used as a regular roost. However, I was very surprised to count 16 birds coming into roost this evening, mostly females but certainly one well-marked male.

February
12th

Rain throughout the day was the first for several weeks but today was dismal. Sixty siskins were feeding on the path between the reedbed and Thorpe Meare, presumably picking up fallen alder seed. Several hoop-petticoat narcissus (native to mountain pastures in south-west Europe and north-west Africa) were in flower at River Hundred, bringing a touch of welcome colour to a grey winter's day.

Hoop-petticoat narcissus at River Hundred

Photo: Kathy Archibald

13th

The birds are under the impression that spring has arrived with several species in full voice, especially the thrushes and tits. Two woodlarks were singing in the air at Stonehouse Common – this month is usually a good time to see these delightful small larks in song, although they only perform in mild, bright conditions. The hazel catkins in Church Wood looked an absolute picture.

Hazel catkins in Church Wood   *Photo:* Rob Macklin

Very mild today with prolonged sunshine throughout the afternoon. Wild arum is now pushing up in the hedgerows and I found my second flowering dandelion, this one on the grazing marshes.

Dandelion, on the grazing marshes

Photo: Rob Macklin

February

Tundra bean geese   *Photo:* Steve Valentine

I carried out a full wildfowl count of the marshes in the afternoon and was delighted to see that 145 white-fronted geese had returned after several days' absence.

They were extremely difficult to count accurately as they were feeding behind the high ground in the north-west corner of the marsh. The small flock of tundra bean geese were feeding on South Marsh, the first time I had ever seen them on that marsh!

Duck numbers seemed to be holding up well with over 3,000 wigeon, 170 gadwall and over 100 handsome shoveler in full breeding plumage.

Three female marsh harriers and a sparrowhawk were disturbing the roosting waders and over 1,000 lapwings were continually in the air. The wheeling flock of 700 dunlin flashed through the sky, their dark upperparts contrasting with brilliant white underparts in a dazzling display.

As I reached the north end of the marshes I flushed two pairs of muntjacs, the dark males looking particularly impressive with their stumpy but sharp antlers.

Drake shoveler in full breeding plumage
Photo: Steve Valentine

13

Tawny owl, more often heard than seen   *Photo:* Stuart Elsom

Earlier in the day I was cleaning out nestboxes on the Walks and I'm not sure who was more surprised when I disturbed a tawny owl from a thicket of recently planted pines in Margaret Wood! Tawny owls are quite abundant here but more often heard than seen.There seemed to be fresh activity around the badger sett with fresh tracks in the soil which had been heaped up by the sett entrance.

February
18th

A hard overnight frost was followed by dense fog which finally cleared to leave a typical sunny, winter's day. Thirty siskins were feeding in the alders by Skinny's Bridge. I flipped open a nestbox to clean it out and was startled to find a wood mouse peering back at me – I replaced the lid and left it well alone. I walked along the south bank of the reedbed, finding a substantial pile of fishy-smelling otter spraint – no sign of any animals though. A fox peered inquisitively at me from the south side of the Hundred river before going about his usual business. Honeysuckle is now well into leaf and the coconut smell from the gorse flowers gave a tantalising promise of spring.

Foxes are common at North Warren   *Photo:* Kathy Archibald

*The word March comes from the Roman "Martius"
and was named after Mars, the god of war.
The Anglo-Saxons called March "Hlyd Monath"
which means month of storms!*

*One of the flowers most associated with March is
the wild daffodil (Narcissus). It is also known as
the Lent lily because it flowers in early spring with
the blooms usually dropping before Easter.
It is the main daffodil species of Britain.*

Daffodils in flower at Aldringham Church   *Photo:* Rob Macklin

March

8th & 9th

San Francisco, USA

I found myself on family business in California in late February and early March but still found time to explore the greener side of San Francisco. The botanical gardens are on the west side of the city and form a part of the Golden Gate Park, providing a green lung for the city. The gardens host a wealth of plants from Asia, Australasia, South America, South Africa and, of course, California.

My first visit was rather brief in the mid-morning sunshine and grey squirrels pleaded for hand-outs from all the visitors – very successfully too. It appeared that these animals were smaller and browner than those in the UK.

Grey squirrels appeared smaller and browner than those in the UK

Photo: Rob Macklin

Stunning California quail   *Photo:* Rob Macklin

Stunning California quails were incredibly tame and western scrub-jays also approached closely to see what was on offer. Several ravens wheeled overhead, accompanied by a soaring red-tailed hawk, and a vociferous red-shouldered hawk flashed through the trees.

Western scrub-jays approached closely   *Photo:* Rob Macklin

I returned in the late afternoon for a more in-depth look at the birds. A commotion in the trees alerted me to a red-shouldered hawk which had caught and killed a large rat, rendering the bird oblivious to my presence.

A red-shouldered hawk was oblivious to my presence   *Photo: Rob Macklin*

A California towhee perched out in the open and a small group of golden-crowned sparrows unconcernedly searched for food on the ground. Several American robins were in the taller trees with one or two in full song; the scrub below them held Townsend's warbler, Hutton's vireo and several yellow-rumped warblers. Some spring flowers were already in flower and these attracted several iridescent Anna's hummingbirds – a delight to watch as they buzzed from flower to flower. Another small bird caught my eye, this one a black-throated gray warbler, and a small foraging flock of bushtits moved through the scrub. On the way back to the house I encountered a throng of birds around a discarded take-away, all scrabbling for crumbs. I was able to identify great-tailed grackles and Brewer's blackbirds, plus the more familiar house sparrows and starlings.

The following sunny morning I paid my third visit to the gardens. The spring flowers had attracted several of the very similar Anna's and Allen's hummingbirds which buzzed from plant to plant. Chestnut-backed chickadees seemed fairly abundant and I had a very close view of a hermit thrush. A great blue heron flew languorously overhead, a violet-green swallow hawked for insects and a sharp-shinned hawk (very similar to our sparrowhawk) soared high in the sky. I walked into an area of coast redwood trees (*Sequoia sempervirens*) where I noted a California song sparrow, a house finch in full song and had a good view of a ruby-crowned kinglet.

My last visit included exploring a wider area of the Golden Gate Park surrounding the gardens although I was aware of threatening cloud and impending rain. As I walked through the gardens I had a very close view of an Oregon dark-eyed junco and a redstart-like black phoebe.

Approaching a large lake I heard a nuthatch calling which turned out to be a pygmy nuthatch and a cedar waxwing perched up unconcernedly above my head. Two large brown woodpecker-like birds on a pile of chippings were northern flickers. On the lake were hundreds of gulls, several Canada geese and at least six pied-billed grebes. As I feared, the rain began to fall and I headed back to the city.

San Franscico Botanical Gardens hold a wealth of plants   *Photo:* Rob Macklin

20

March
15th

T he "Ides of March" in the Roman calendar and the day on which the month was divided into two equal parts. Julius Caesar was murdered on this date in 44 BC.

16th

Curlew – found on marshes and heath   *Photo:* Mark Breaks

S till bitterly cold on the Suffolk coast with a lazy, easterly wind (lazy because it goes through you, not around you) and temperatures barely above freezing. Snowdrops provided a splash of colour in the poplar wood and at Sheepwash Crossing but precious little else was in flower. At River Hundred the introduced hoop-petticoat narcissus is in full bloom while least narcissus is now poking through. A small flock of 16 curlews were feeding on the acid grassland heath.

21

Otter on the River Hundred – they have returned with a vengeance

Photo: Kathy Archibald

I came across a clump of three mature alders that had fallen across the river, providing an opportunistic bridge for foxes and the like! Otters have returned to the reedbed with a vengeance; I found two huge piles of fresh spraint plus two smaller deposits on the reedbed bank. A female marsh harrier drifted slowly over the reeds.

23rd

Sunny and cold all day with the wind moving around to the south-east. Still no sign of any spring migrant birds but a few of the resident species were tempted into song. At least 100 lapwings were feeding on the short acid grassland on the heath with another 110 on the same habitat at Snape Warren later in the afternoon.

22

Lapwings forage on heath and marshes   *Photo:* Stuart Elsom

25th

Spring arrives at last as the wind turns to the south-west and temperatures reach the dizzy heights of the mid-teens! A pair of marsh harriers display over the reedbed, skydiving and twisting in the air. I find my first ladybird.

26th

Two singing chiffchaffs at Church Farm Wood were my first spring migrants, a full ten days later than expected. A linnet was also in song. Still a great many snowdrops in flower at Aldringham Church and Sheepwash Crossing. My first bumble bee of the year was a ginger-brown (*Bombus pascuorum*) taking nectar from snowdrops in Church Wood. The woods were full of redwings and blackbirds taking on much-needed fuel for the long flight back to northern Europe. Our own breeding male blackbirds have yellow bills by now, distinguishing them from their black-billed Continental cousins.

I flushed four woodcocks from the birch woods and surprised a "spring" of four teal on the ponds at River Hundred. A red admiral was taking advantage of the sun reflecting off the white walls of the house.

One of "our own" adult male blackbirds   *Photo:* Richard Thomas

Water rail at the reedbed edge. A total of 35 territories was discovered here.
Photo: Stuart Elsom

28th

An early morning visit to the reedbed to carry out a water rail survey using a tape lure; I was able to identify 35 breeding territories which was an excellent result in the strong south-westerly winds. Six marsh harriers over the reeds included two displaying pairs, the birds calling high in the air before plunging down towards the reeds; an inquisitive immature male was quickly seen off by one of the resident males. A stunning male hen harrier flew low over the reeds having to dodge the attentions of an adult female peregrine falcon – an amazing morning for raptors!

Two Cetti's warblers sang from either end of the reedbed and four sand martins searching for insects low over the reeds were the first of the year. Four red deer, including a young male, were feeding on the emerging rushes but bolted off through the reedbed on my approach. More signs of spring included a toad croaking from one of the dykes plus small tortoiseshell and red admiral butterflies on the wing.

30th

The first lesser celandines are in flower below Bird's Farm. Still mild and windy – woodcocks now moving through in numbers with four in the garden today.

March

Lesser celandines at Bird's Farm   *Photo:* Rob Macklin

31st

My first comma butterfly of the year in Rendlesham Forest. The butterfly is so named, not for its brilliant colouration, but for the presence of a small white "comma" mark on the underside of the hind wings. In Suffolk this species was considered a great rarity throughout the 19th Century and until the 1930s but now can be encountered anywhere in the county! Blackthorn out in flower along the Sizewell Road and there is a splendid patch of red dead-nettle showing at Ness House. An alpine swift was reported over Sizewell village.

Comma butterfly, above, and red
dead-nettle at Ness House, right
Photos: Rob Macklin

No one knows for certain how April got its name, but it may have come from the Latin word "Aperire" meaning "to open". April is the month in the northern hemisphere when the buds begin to open and plants grow again after winter.

The Anglo-Saxon name for April was "Eastremonath" and the name of the Christian festival of Easter comes from this.

1st

All Fools Day! Spring is late this year, the elder bushes just coming into leaf. Several white-tailed bumblebees (*Bombus lucorum*) were around the house while both small tortoiseshell and comma butterflies were active at River Hundred.

The First of April, some do say
Is set apart for All Fools Day;
But why the people call it so,
Not I, nor they themselves do know.

Small tortoiseshell, active at River Hundred   Photo: Rob Macklin

27

Early swallow over North Warren   *Photo:* Peter Beesley

2nd

Another woodcock shot out of the dense bracken in the birch woods and the second swallow of the spring hawked for insects over the reedbed. A red-tailed bumblebee (*Bombus lapidarius*) buzzed over the heath on the Walks.

Adder; three were basking in the sunshine   *Photo:* Nicola Breaks

5th

A gloriously sunny, if cold, spring morning with frost on the ground. I looked for woodlarks on the heath but to no avail. I did find several shelducks already prospecting for nest burrows and 27 curlews feeding in the short turf.

Looking for Dartford warblers in the deep heather at River Hundred I almost stumbled over three adders basking in the sunshine. Two were almost black and the third a much lighter brown, probably two males and a lighter female – all were about two feet in length!

Looked for lapwings on the marshes this afternoon, although it was still cold and breezy. The birds were particularly quiet, only rousing themselves to see off the occasional passing carrion crow. Six tundra bean geese remained on the marshes – unusual as they normally leave in February! The remnants of the winter duck population included 300 wigeon, 127 teal and a few shoveler. Just three pairs of gadwall and a single pair of pintail were on the marshes – the gadwall will stay to breed but the pintails will fly north to their breeding grounds.

Oystercatcher.
A pair has taken up
residence in the
north pools
Photo: Stuart Elsom

A solitary little egret fished along the dykes, a calling whimbrel went over and a pair of oystercatchers have taken up residence at the north pools.

Two male bitterns were booming loudly in the reedbed and two pairs of marsh harriers drifted slowly over the reedtops – amazing to consider that in 1971 there was only one breeding pair in the UK, at nearby Minsmere. In 2006 marsh harriers fledged 27 young at Minsmere, a tremendously successful conservation story.

A bittern stands tall. Two males were booming in the reedbed
Photo: John Archibald

30

April
14th

Warmer today with long periods of sunshine and temperatures up to 15°C. I completed the breeding lapwing survey on the marshes, finding 26 pairs and at least seven active nests. Lapwings are now largely confined to coastal grazing marshes in east Suffolk, the arable nesting birds long since gone as winter-sown crops replaced spring-sown. Redshank numbers are building up and two pairs of avocets look to be interested in South Marsh. A stunning male wheatear was inspecting rabbit burrows on the rabbit-grazed heath overlooking the marshes. They seem to do this every year before moving on!

Several butterflies on the wing included commas, small tortoiseshells and peacocks. Ground ivy is just coming into flower on the heath at River Hundred. Bluebell leaves are through, but still a long way from flowering.

Wheatears are regular spring visitors to North Warren   *Photo:* Stuart Elsom

Spring has sprung when the first nightingale is heard   *Photo: Stuart Elsom*

15th

Spring is really here when the first nightingale is heard and one was singing loudly from dense cover in Alexander Wood early this morning. This cherished summer visitor has decreased in range and numbers over recent years, although the Suffolk coast remains a breeding stronghold. My first whitethroat of the year was singing at the rear of Aldringham Church.

Perhaps more surprising was a singing male lesser redpoll on the west side of Alexander Wood, accompanied by two females. Many of the recently arrived linnets are now settling down to breed, although a 100-strong flock was still looking for seeds on fallow land by Square Covert.

April
17th

S aw my first frog of the year, a really large individual clambering over the boardwalk through the fen. An alder tree had fallen across the River Hundred and a kingfisher flashed away upstream as I approached – an exhilarating sight! A single pair always nest at North Warren and they used to breed in the root-plate of an upturned tree at River Hundred.

An alder tree had fallen
across the river
Photo: Rob Macklin

Kingfishers always nest at North Warren   *Photo:* John Archibald

A red kite flew over the Warren   *Photo:* Stuart Elsom

An excellent day for migrants with both red kite and goshawk over the Warren and a pair of exquisite little ringed plovers on a pool on North Marsh. A small group of yellow wagtails on South Marsh included a pair of blue-headed wagtails, overshooting visitors from southern Europe.

A pair of blue-headed wagtails had overshot from southern Europe

Photo: Stuart Elsom

The first house martin of the year skimmed over the marshes and another first, a green-veined white butterfly, was in the garden at River Hundred. The willow catkins are in full flower, attracting peacock butterflies and hordes of honey bees.

The first green-veined
white of the year was
in the garden
Photo: Rob Macklin

Peacock butterflies were on the willow catkins   *Photo:* Rob Macklin

April
18th

Blythburgh Church, the "Cathedral of the Marshes", looked spectacular, towering over the wet lowland landscape   *Photo:* Rob Macklin

Walked along the river from Blythburgh, across the marshes to Blyford Bridge; the "Cathedral of the Marshes", as Blythburgh Church is colloquially known, looked spectacular, towering over the wet lowland landscape. The fields were quite rank and undergrazed, attracting very few birds apart from one solitary pair of oystercatchers. A substantial group of waders, mainly bar-tailed godwits and dunlin, was feeding on the mud on the estuary. More spring flowers were apparent along the roadside, particularly dandelion, lesser celandine and red deadnettle.

At Blyford Bridge a herd of Jersey cattle made a fine sight grazing the meadows against a backdrop of the church. Goldfinches and a treecreeper sang from the riverside oak trees and a kingfisher streaked away down the river. I was then greeted with an astonishing sight – a huge fish, over two feet long, was battling its way up the tidal river. The river was very shallow so the fish was half in and half out of the water! Pale spots along the side of the fish seemed to suggest that it was a sea trout coming back to spawn in our coastal rivers after many years in the oceans.

A herd of Jersey cattle made a fine sight at Blyford Bridge   *Photo:* Rob Macklin

Top: I was astounded to find a
stone-curlew   *Photo:* Mark Breaks

Right: Rank grassland at
Abbey Farm   *Photo:* Rob Macklin

In the afternoon I took the opportunity to have another look around Abbey Farm at Snape. Several snipe were feeding on the edge of a flight pond and spiralled up and away as I approached. A grass snake slipped silently into the cover of the grass. There was no sign of the lapwings I had seen earlier in the month but I was astounded to find a stone-curlew superbly camouflaged amongst the vegetation on the fallow fields. It flew a short way, showing off the distinctive black and white patches in the wings. It then settled close to the ground and I was able to watch it from the banks of the Alde river. A Cetti's warbler sang from dense cover on the river edge.

42

April

19th

"Angel's tears" were in full, brilliant flower   *Photo:* Rob Macklin

Sand martins have arrived back at their breeding colony at Thorpeness Common; further erosion over the winter has left the cliffs sheer and perfect for excavating new holes in the soft sand.

A nightingale sang from the back of the allotments at Thorpeness and several pairs of yellowhammers were busy nesting in the gorse on the common. Mistle and song thrushes are singing constantly in the garden at River Hundred and "angel's tears" daffodils are in full, brilliant flower.

20th

On the way into Minsmere I saw 40 red deer grazing unconcernedly on the new grass of the recently converted arable fields. Many more nightingales today!

A herd of red deer grazed on the new grass of the converted arable fields
Photo: Rob Macklin

22nd

Walked up Nuttery Lane and around the back of Chapel Farm looking for, and failing to find, any singing woodlarks. Plenty of skylarks were singing over the cereal fields and green woodpeckers called from Old Broom and Miller's Covert. Heard my second cuckoo of the year! The high ground here allows superb views across the Alde estuary.

Kestrel and sparrowhawk were hunting over the golfcourse while the dense scrub supported singing blackcap, whitethroat, willow warbler and chiffchaff. White climbing fumitory now in flower.

23rd

St. George's Day – England's national day! The emblem of St. George, a red cross on a white background, was adopted by Richard the Lionheart and brought to England in the 12th Century. The king's soldiers wore it on their tunics to avoid any confusion in battle!

Male sparrowhawk, a much-maligned predator   *Photo:* Graham Catley

Dense fog shrouded the marshes as I attempted to search for breeding redshanks and very little activity was apparent. Six little egrets were feeding in the shallows and four black-tailed godwits were taking on more fuel for their long journey north to Iceland. I came across the remains of a dead fox on South Marsh then surprised a sparrowhawk on the body of a lapwing – a most unfortunate choice of victim! Sparrowhawks almost disappeared from Suffolk in the 1960s and 1970s due to the introduction of chemicals and pesticides such as DDT. However, restrictions on the use of these insidious chemicals allowed the species to recover and it is now common along the Suffolk coast. The species is widely blamed for decimating songbird populations, although research has shown this to be totally untrue. The females are much larger than the males and are able to tackle prey such as magpies, jays and woodpigeons.

Still 50 siskins feeding in the birches at River Hundred and lesser stitchwort now coming into flower. Checked out the majority of the nestboxes on the reserve this afternoon; many blue and great tits have now started laying their clutches.The fog has barely lifted all day!

April
25th

Driving back from Norwich I saw three "white hart" fallow deer on the edge of the woods at Henham. Fallow deer were re-introduced into Britain by the Normans at the end of the 11th Century as fossil records show they were present before the last ice age. They were known as "Beasts of the Forest" and hence they belonged to the king! Fallow deer are common in Tunstall and Rendlesham Forests but are largely replaced by reed deer at Dunwich and Minsmere.

'White hart' – a white fallow deer with a conventional stag   *Photo: Jim Law*

27th

Garden warblers and lesser whitethroats are now arriving in encouraging numbers as early summer really gathers pace. A pair of avocets are still on South Marsh so hopefully they will stay to breed. Two very noisy and aggressive pairs of oystercatchers might help out by driving off any marauding jackdaws and carrion crows.

Grasshopper warblers are more easily heard than seen   *Photo:* Graham Catley

I heard my first grasshopper warbler "reeling" on the edge of South Marsh. This is an exceptionally difficult bird to see in the field but can easily be located by its distinctive song, likened by some to the sound of a fishing reel!

On the higher, sandy ground above the marshes I encountered a patch of cowslips which had produced over 50 flowering spikes from just 12 plants. Nearby three male and two female wheatears were investigating rabbit burrows – they were not as bright as the earlier birds and were probably of the "Greenland" race. They will not stay! Lesser stitchwort is in full flower along the old railway track, which will attract green-veined white butterflies. The first speckled wood of the year at River Hundred.

Cowslips at North Warren and, below, lesser stitchwort along the old railway track

Photos: Rob Macklin

29th

Sizewell Common was alive with the sound of singing willow and garden warblers, even though it was still cold in a brisk north-easterly wind. Cow parsley now in flower and green alkanet out by Home Farm.

May

> *May is named after the Greek goddess Maia and is a time of great celebration in the northern hemisphere. In Britain May Day marked the end of the harsh winter months and welcomed the beginning of summer.*
>
> *The Anglo-Saxon name for May was "Tri-Milchi" in recognition that cows could be milked three times a day with the advent of lush, verdant pastures.*

1st

Heavy overnight rain continued throughout the morning. May Day (also known as Garland Day) was a major annual festival celebrated with music, dancing and games. May Day celebrations have their origins in the Roman festival of Flora, goddess of fruit and flowers, which marked the beginning of summer. Maypole dancing was another traditional pursuit on May Day.

The first of May is Garland Day
So please remember the garland.
We don't come here but once a year,
So please remember the garland

2nd

Checked out the bitterns in the reedbed then carried out a full wader survey on the grazing marshes. Two male bitterns were booming strongly from the depths of the reedbed while both pairs of marsh harriers were very active, intent on dodging the attentions of several carrion crows. Several Cetti's warblers were in full, strident song around the edges of the marshes, sedge warbler numbers seemed to be up and reed warblers had just begun to make their presence felt.

Avocets were feeding in the shallow pools on the grazing marsh

Photo: Stuart Elsom

A lone grasshopper warbler was reeling away from dense cover on the east edge of South Marsh.

Six avocets were feeding in the shallow pools on the grazing marshes. Both lapwing and redshank numbers were encouraging and an oystercatcher nest has appeared on the islands on the north pools. No lapwing chicks as yet!

Just one cuckoo heard today.

Butterflies were very thin on the ground although I did find the first two large-red damselflies of the year. Garlic mustard out in flower on the upper banks of the Hundred river.

The storm of October 1987 gave rise to excellent breeding opportunities for woodlarks
in Rendlesham and Tunstall Forests   *Photo: Stuart Elsom*

3rd

Sunny all day and the winds have finally swung around to the south. The forecasters are promising temperatures will hit the low 20s in the next few days!

An early start enlivened by warblers singing from every rough patch of bramble and scrub. Several nightingales were singing beautifully on the Walks, promising a good year for this fantastic songster. I flushed a woodlark from its nest which was well hidden in bracken under heather; the female feigned injury as she left the nest and I saw four brownish eggs neatly arranged in a cup lined with fine grasses. Woodlarks were extremely scarce on the Suffolk coast until the great storm in October 1987. The severe destruction of Rendlesham and Tunstall Forests and subsequent re-planting provided excellent breeding opportunities for woodlarks. In 2006 numbers had reached a very respectable 176 pairs.

Many linnets have now taken up breeding territories, although there was still a flock of 130 birds on fallow land on the north side of Square Covert. A classic sound of summer was delivered by three "purring" turtle doves on the Walks.

Two speckled wood butterflies were spiralling up madly together – so intense was their rivalry that they were completely oblivious to my presence.

My first hobby of the year was hawking for insects over the reedbed while the very pale male marsh harrier was calling and skydiving over the reedbed and heath.

Three wheatears of the "Greenland" race were in full splendour on the sandy heath overlooking the marshes and a female whinchat perched up in the scrub along the old railway track. Still very few cuckoos.

Orange-tip and green hairstreak butterflies were on the wing at River Hundred and cuckoo flower was out in the fen. It is also known as lady's-smock, which is more expressive as the flowers vary in colour from very pale pink to mauve and are slightly cupped or "frocked".

Cuckoo flower was out in the fen   *Photo:* Rob Macklin

52

May
4th

A glorious sunny spring day with temperatures in the low 20s and a southerly breeze. Walked up into Alexander and Margaret Wood on the Walks where at least eight nightingales were in song. Whitethroat numbers were less than expected in Margaret Wood but, perversely, lesser whitethroats appeared to be more numerous than usual. Two young red deer stags gazed apprehensively at me from deep cover before making off. Both had knobs on the top of their heads where the new antlers were beginning to form. Twenty-two greylag geese were feeding out in the open on winter barley.

The first brood of great tits appeared in a nestbox at River Hundred; the oaks are not yet in leaf so finding enough winter moth caterpillars for the young may be difficult. The birch trees are just coming into leaf.

There is a profusion of ground ivy in flower over parts of the grassland at North Warren while, in the fen, marsh marigolds are poking their yellow heads through the dry reed stems.

Marsh marigolds peeped through the dry reed stems   *Photo:* Rob Macklin

Ground ivy in flower at Snape Warren and,
inset, beech flowers at North Warren

Photos: Rob Macklin

5th

Another superb spring day, making it a joy to walk over Snape Warren. One area which had been cleared of bracken was carpeted in a colourful array of sheep's sorrel, ground ivy, early forget-me-not, white climbing fumitory and dove's-foot cranesbill. I counted eight singing woodlarks taking full advantage of the balmy conditions, singing from high in the sky.

A lesser whitethroat sang from the wooded area and just one nightingale gave voice from the edge of Snape Marshes.

There was a superb array of Russian comfrey along the footpath on the south side of Snape Maltings. At River Hundred the beech trees were in flower.

May
6th

Large numbers of house martins and swifts arrived today, hunting for insects in the skies over the wetlands at the Warren. Turtle doves are also beginning to trickle in.

I found a splendid array of bur chervil in flower along the western edge of Sizewell Common.

7th

Dreary low cloud brought much-needed rain throughout the day. Two bitterns were booming enthusiastically in the reedbed and a male marsh harrier brought in food for one of the females. Most of the breeding blue tits and great tits in the nestboxes have full clutches of eggs.

A great tit nest with six eggs in a nestbox   *Photo:* Rob Macklin

May
8th

White climbing fumitory has carpeted the floor of Square Covert and will flourish until the bracken comes through. Heavy rain throughout the afternoon.

9th

An early haze soon gave way to bright sunshine and a really warm day. Hawthorn flowers were out in Little Beauties Wood and I found a fully developed wild arum, commonly known as "Lords and Ladies" or Cuckoo Pint, vivid lime green against the leaf litter. This spectacular plant has long associations with East Anglia.

"Old fenmen in the last century held the traditional belief that when the nuns came over from Normandy to build a convent at Thetford in Norfolk they brought with them the wild arum or cuckoo pint.

When the monks of Ely stole the body of St. Withburga from East Dereham, and paused, on their way back, to rest at Brandon, tradition has it that the nuns of Thetford came down to the riverside and covered the saint's body with the flowers.

During the long journey down the Little Ouse of the barge bearing St. Withburga several of the flowers fell into the river, where they threw out roots.

Within an hour they had covered all the banks as far as Ely with a carpet of blooms, and more remarkable still, these flowers glowed radiantly at night."

E. M. Porter,
Cambridgeshire Customs and
Folklore, 1969

Wild arum coming into flower   *Photo:* Rob Macklin

Lord and Ladies berry spike   *Photo:* Rob Macklin

My first four-spotted chaser dragonfly sped through Church Walk – several more were out at North Warren later in the day.

A hobby was soaring high over Church Wood and a further four were hawking for St. Mark's flies over the reedbed. Both pairs of marsh harriers were in the air together with the dark male skydiving and calling, a tremendous spectacle!

Thousands of St. Mark's flies were attracted to the sweet, coconut-scented gorse, broom and blackthorn flowers. Two dazzlingly fresh hairy dragonflies were on the bank of gorse by Peggy's Perch, one of them feeding on yet another unfortunate St. Mark's fly!

Broom in flower at North Warren　　*Photo:* Rob Macklin

Spring brings grazing animals on to the heath and 34 Manx Loghtan sheep arrived at the Warren today. These are a very scarce rare breed from the Isle of Man and we have found them invaluable in controlling invasive scrub and grass – they also look extraordinary! The only problem with this breed is that they do not "flock" like normal sheep and tend to disappear in all directions when it is time to move them.

58

Manx Loghtan sheep are invaluable in controlling invasive scrub and grass
Photo: Rob Macklin

The profusion of apple, pear and cherry blossom this year is truly something to behold! The local growers maintain that long, steady periods of cold weather throughout the winter are responsible for this spectacular show.

Apple blossom in Church Wood, part of a show that is truly something to behold

Photo: Rob Macklin

May

Cherry blossom at Bird's Farm, the spectacular show of blossom is said to be the result of long, steady cold periods in the winter   *Photo:* Rob Macklin

The dry, sandy grassland overlooking the marshes is a carpet of pink dove's-foot cranesbill and blue early forget-me-not. Ochreous sulphur-tuft fungus sprouted out of the base of an oak tree in the woods.

Insects are now becoming more obvious – the first azure blue damselfly was on the wing today and green-veined whites were common along the old railway track, taking advantage of the masses of flowering lesser stitchwort. The first holly blue of the summer was on a huge rhododendron bush at River Hundred.

Where are all the cuckoos?

May 10th

Church Common, Snape, a wild corner of the Sandlings   Photo: Rob Macklin

A fabulous early summer day, cloudless skies and a light easterly breeze. A pair of avocets have settled down on the north pools and it would appear that the female has a nest on one of the islands. The lapwings spend their days chasing passing carrion crows, jackdaws and gulls, which suggests they have vulnerable young to protect. A fox was on the edge of the Hundred river at the back of the pools.

Church Common at Snape is a wild corner of the Sandlings heaths surrounded by an intensively farmed landscape. Rough grassland and clumps of sweet-smelling gorse have attracted breeding whitethroats and linnets and an amazing density of singing skylarks. Rabbits have made their mark here by excavating holes and providing patches of bare ground.

61

Walked in the south of Tunstall Forest looking for singing woodlarks; garden warblers and yellowhammers were in full song and a striking green woodpecker flew overhead uttering its strident "yaffle" call. The windrows are still very much in evidence, lines of dead conifers piled up after the 1987 storm; they make superb hibernation sites for adders.

Windrows in Tunstall Forest are still very much in evidence
Photo: Rob Macklin

I came across a glorious patch of bluebells which had managed to push their way through the dead bracken fronds, under and around several large beech trees. What a contrast between the open area of bluebells with the darkness and gloom under the tightly-packed rows of spruce trees. Two green hairstreaks spiralled up in the air together in dispute, oblivious to the world around them. The males are very territorial and aerial battles take place frequently as they defend their territories. The same perches may be used year after year by successive generations. A queen red-tailed bumble bee sampled the nectar from the gorse flowers.

Bluebells in bracken in Tunstall Forest
Photo: Rob Macklin

May

Iken Church is a very special place – a church with craftsmanship spanning a thousand years, in a scene as serene and memorable as that of any Suffolk church. Founded by St. Botolph in 654 it commands a majestic view of the River Alde and has survived a devastating raid by the Danes in 870 and a disastrous fire on April 4th 1968.

Iken Church – a very special place   *Photo:* Rob Macklin

Churchyard management was being carried out by four very contented-looking Suffolk sheep, while blackcaps and goldcrests sang from the wilder corners of the churchyard. Why does every old church have a yew tree? Yew trees were long held sacred by the pagan folk and these places of worship were taken on by the Christian church to provide continuity for the local population.

Churchyard management was being carried out by Suffolk sheep
Photo: Rob Macklin

A magnificent yew tree in the churchyard
Photo:
Rob Macklin

One corner of the churchyard effervesced with flowering cow parsley and several noisy pairs of jackdaws appeared to be nesting in the neighbouring house, "Anchorage".

Masses of herb robert now in flower along the old railway track and I saw my first flowering red campion.

64

Common whitethroat on Thorpeness Common   *Photo:* Richard Thomas

A morning on the local commons starting at Thorpeness Common where a stunning yellow wagtail was searching for food on the short rabbit-grazed turf. The surrounding scrub was alive with singing whitethroats and garden warblers.

Fifty sand martins were buzzing along the severely eroded clifftop and excitedly going in and out of the many freshly excavated nest holes – I counted 115 new ones! A nearby fallow field was a colourful array of native "arable weeds", a derogoratory term for such splendid plants, as well as recent alien introductions such as spring beauty (from California) and amsinckia, also known as common fiddleneck, which arrived in the country as an impurity in crop seed from North America. A redeeming feature of spring beauty is that it can be collected and eaten as a salad or as a cooked vegetable.

Sand martins
were buzzing
along the
Thorpeness cliffs
Photo: John Davies

On to Stonehouse Common where lesser whitethroats and willow warblers were singing well – such a joyous spring sound. As the day warmed up butterflies began to emerge and I soon noted holly blue, comma and green hairstreak; the latter has decreased markedly in recent years, seeming to prefer warm, dry springs.

Green hairstreak on bramble flowers   *Photo:* Rob Macklin

66

Sizewell Common hosted more singing whitethroats, linnets and yellowhammers and just one nightingale singing beautifully. This year has seen more nightingales than in recent years particularly in the small woods dotted across the landscape at Aldringham Walks. A lone female marsh harrier flew north being escorted away by a watchful carrion crow.

On all three commons thousands of St. Mark's flies had descended on to the gorse flowers and bramble scrub.

Later in the afternoon I paid a visit to Foxburrow Wood, a remnant of ancient woodland in an agricultural landscape. Two brown hares loped unconcernedly across the neighbouring cornfield. The wood was awash in a sea of spectacular flowering bluebells whose delicate scent was overwhelmed in places by the astringent, garlic scent of starry-white ramsons. Also known as wild garlic, places were named after its Old English root *hrmsa* including Ramsholt on the River Deben! Despite their strong smell ramsons are surprisingly mild to eat and can be used in salads, soups or just eaten raw! Spikes of primroses and purple bugle adorned the track edge under the gaze of towering oaks and many field maples.

Bluebells in Foxburrow Wood, above, and inset, ransoms on the woodland floor

Photos: Rob Macklin

Bugle spikes in flower   *Photo:* Rob Macklin

15th

Went up to Theberton Wood this afternoon where several of the surrounding fields are reverting naturally back to scrub and woodland. Some of the hedges here are a thick tangle of field maple, oak, hazel, white poplar, hawthorn, blackthorn and bramble providing ideal nest sites for whitethroats and long-tailed tits. A small flock of 12 stock doves flew up from the corner of one of the smaller fields.

Ancient
hedgerow at
Theberton Wood
Photo: Rob Macklin

The woodland floor was carpeted in dog's mercury, wood sedge and lots of ash and hazel saplings. Large patches of bluebells and bugle were prominent while primroses lit up the ground flora. Sanicle was also very prolific and there were patches of common dog-violets, barren strawberry and piercing blue germander speedwell. Figwort was also abundant here, but not yet in flower, and I was lucky enough to find three flowering spikes of early purple orchid. Blackbirds, chiffchaffs and blackcaps were all in glorious song.

Early purple orchid in Theberton Wood   *Photo:* Rob Macklin

69

May
16th

Small copper   *Photo:* Richard Thomas

Walked across Snape Warren this morning; garden warblers were singing their delightful, melodic songs and I watched a male great-spotted woodpecker searching for insects on the bark of a silver birch. The dark reds of sheep's sorrel dominate the open grassland with eyebright in full flower and heath bedstraw just coming out. White flowers on the rowan trees are also coming through. Sparkling small copper butterflies were taking advantage of the warm conditions. On the open grass I found a small group of pheasant eggs which had been eaten by predators, probably carrion crows.

A bright green woodpecker was feeding out on the open grassland and a tawny owl called from the nearby birch wood. Willow warblers filled the air with their liquid, candescent song and a snatch of nightingale song came from dense cover in the wood. A few pairs of oystercatchers and redshanks were nesting on the saltmarsh bordering the River Alde, their piping calls carrying far over the heath. I heard a cuckoo!

A Dartford warbler rattled out its dry, staccato song from a dense clump of gorse on the highest point of the Warren, soon joined by the fluty notes of a woodlark which were delivered from high up in the sky. After an absence of 60 years one or two pairs of Dartford warblers returned to breed on the Sandlings in 1996 and the population now stands at a healthy 117 pairs. This perky, little warbler can now be found on many of the gorse-clad heaths on the Suffolk coast between Walberswick and Felixstowe.

The perky Dartford warbler has returned to the Suffolk coast   *Photo:* Mark Breaks

18th

O vernight rain and storms gave way to a bright and breezy morning so I decided to work my way around the reedbed, braving the waist-high nettles. Both male marsh harriers were quartering the area and the darker male brought in prey for one of the females. The female in question rose from deep cover and took the prey from the male in a spectacular "aerial pass" before descending back into the dense reeds! Three hobbies were furiously hunting dragonflies and other smaller insects low over the reeds and they were joined by swifts, sand martins and several black-headed gulls. Two male bitterns boomed softly from the depths of the reedbed.

As I battled my way through the dense nettlebeds on the south bank of the reedbed I disturbed thousands of damselflies, estimating at least 640 large red damselflies which were far outnumbered by bright blue azure damselflies. A few hairy dragonflies were in the air although large numbers of four-spotted chasers were sheltering from the wind amongst the nettles.

Large red damselfly
Photo:
Rob Macklin

Four-spotted chaser
Photo:
Rob Macklin

72

The reedbed was alive with breeding birds seemingly excited about the new season. Several reed buntings were singing in full view and bearded tits could be heard "pinging" from the reeds. Reed warblers provided a continuous backdrop of sound and at least two Cetti's warblers attempted to be heard over the cacophony!

> *"What would the world be, once bereft*
> *Of wet and wildness? Let them be left,*
> *O let them be left, wildness and wet,*
> *Long live the weeds and the wildness yet."*
>
> *Gerald Manley Hopkins,*
> Inversnaid

Bogbean, in full flower, had gained a foothold in the reedbed
Photo: John Davies

Reedbeds can be a continuous monoculture but occasionally other plants gain a foothold and at the east end of the reedbed bogbean had come into full flower. I almost trod on a two foot long grass snake which scuttled away through the dense bracken. Red admirals were searching for just the right nettles on which to lay their eggs, peacocks and orange-tips were on the wing and several green hairstreaks were perched up on neighbouring gorse, hawthorn and broom.

73

May

Striped hawk-moth   *Photo:* Robin Harvey

Moth-trapping is carried out almost continuously at Minsmere throughout the summer months and today was a real red-letter day as a striped hawk-moth was found in the trap. The moth trap can catch hundreds of moths which are then examined, identified, and set free.

23rd

A brief respite after four days of strong winds and torrential rain! I decided to visit the grazing marshes to see how our breeding wading birds had fared. As I suspected, all three pairs of avocets had abandoned their nests on the north pools; the eggs were missing, suggesting that they had been removed by predators after the birds had deserted. This was only the second occasion that avocets had nested at North Warren and both attempts had now failed! The lapwings and redshanks had also left the area and the oystercatcher nest had disappeared. A solitary greenshank was feeding in the shallow pools.

A few butterflies had managed to survive the downpour, including a well-worn painted lady which was feeding on hawthorn blossom. A wall brown was sunning itself on the stonework at River Hundred and this was to be one of the few sightings of the year. Two young rabbits had been struck down by the insidious myxamatosis on the old railway track. Three lizards were soaking up the warmth provided by the boardwalk through the fen. Two pollarded ash trees stood sentinel and bare at Bird's Farm.

Pollarded ash trees at Bird's Farm   *Photo:* Rob Macklin

Later in the afternoon a vibrantly colourful knot in full breeding plumage and a black-bellied dunlin were feeding avidly on the muddy edges on South Marsh.

A spotted redshank searched for food   *Photo:* Mark Breaks

Another overcast, grey and dull morning; the weather this May has been abysmal! I searched South Marsh for breeding waders and found nine redshanks and at least eight lapwings but could find no sign of chicks. A common sandpiper looked hungrily for insects in the shallow margins and a spotted redshank searched for food in deeper water.

Another couple of cuckoos have arrived but they are still very thin on the ground. A flock of 40 twittering linnets were looking for seeds on the higher, drier fields. A grey heron was struggling to swallow a large eel it had caught on the marshes and two little egrets were fishing along the dyke edges. Two males and a female tufted duck landed briefly on the main dyke on South Marsh before flying off south.

Red clover is in flower and hedgerow cranesbill is adding a touch of colour along the beach and tracks of the reserve. The hawthorn has finally flowered in all its "May" glory, the venerable specimen at River Hundred looking particularly glorious. The hawthorn, or May-tree, is the only British plant to be named after the month in which it blooms. Its blossoming marks the cusp between spring and summer and the old saying "Cast ne'er a clout 'ere May is out" almost certainly refers to the opening of the flowers and not the end of the month.

The hawthorn,
or May-tree,
has finally
flowered at
River Hundred,
in all its
"May" glory
Photo: Rob Macklin

28th

Many of the small fields around Church Farm at Aldringham have been left fallow this year, providing a haven for a wealth of wildflowers. The fields are full of pink cut-leaved cranesbill, yellow smooth sowthistle and groundsel with occasional patches of common cudweed and striking, blood-red poppies. A nearby field boasted intense blue bugloss, common fiddleneck, common storksbill and the sprawling birdsfoot. The spring hedgerows were ablaze with red and white campion, dove's-foot cranesbill, ground ivy and cow parsley – a riot of colour!

A blood-red poppy below Aldringham Church   *Photo:* Rob Macklin

A skylark, seemingly full of the joys of early summer, sang overhead, a blackcap held forth from a bramble patch and a hobby drifted over. Several swifts hawked for insects around the church.

Slender thistle was coming into flower on the edge of Church Wood and a male orange-tip butterfly was resting on its flower head showing its perfect natural camouflage. Earlier two other males were taking nectar from the yellow sowthistles.

The hedgerows were ablaze with red campion
Photo: Rob Macklin

Male orange-tip showing
camouflaged undersides

Photo: Rob Macklin

I was listening to a nightingale in its operatic performance when I noticed a flock of 30 large finches feeding and calling from a clump of birch trees. Their distinctive *"chup-chup"* calls quickly identified them as crossbills, probably freshly arrived from the Continent. I was able to make out several of the stunning brick-red males before they flew off with their familiar bounding flight. A real find!

Male crossbill – a real find!   *Photo:* Graham Catley

79

May 30th

Lilac in full flower at Sheepwash Crossing   *Photo:* Rob Macklin

Still remarkably chilly with winds from the north bringing extensive heavy showers. Reports suggest this has been the wettest May since 1983. Birdsong is now beginning to tail off although there are still occasional bursts from chiffchaffs, blackcaps, garden warblers and the very vocal Cetti's warblers. Both male marsh harriers were joined by a female over the reedbed and two bitterns continued to boom, although this too is becoming less frequent.

Wood avens brightened up the woods with their bright yellow flowers and two southern marsh orchids are just coming into flower in the fen. The introduced lilac which is very abundant around the edges of the Warren was still in full bloom.

A veteran, gnarled willow tree on the edge of the reedbed supported a splendid array of "chicken of the woods" or sulphur polypore. I took a portion home for supper! I like to parboil it in one inch chunks before sautéing in garlic butter but it is important to collect only young specimens.

"Chicken of the woods" growing on a gnarled willow – I took a portion home for supper!
Photo: Rob Macklin

A severe hailstorm in the early afternoon, the size of marbles!

81

June

> *June marks the beginning of summer in the*
> *northern hemisphere and takes its name from the*
> *Roman goddess Junno, the goddess of marriage.*
>
> *The Anglo Saxons called June "Sera Monath",*
> *the dry month.*

1st

The first day of flaming June – cloud, rain and a cold northerly wind! Checked the nestboxes on the Walks; several had dead chicks after the recent cold weather but many boxes contained young preparing to go or already fledged. Opened one of the nestboxes only to disturb a large hornet that had taken refuge there.

Hornet in nestbox   *Photo:* Rob Macklin

The only two guelder rose bushes on the whole reserve were in flower but look to be in danger of being overwhelmed by the surrounding scrub.

2nd

Up to Snape Warren again this morning – the carpet of sheep's sorrel on the bracken-cleared areas looks an absolute treat. I put up two pairs of woodlarks and the yellowhammers are still singing well.

I moved on to Minsmere, taking in the popular trails around the coastal lagoons or "Scrape" as it is more popularly known. The east hide was full of excited birders watching a real rarity, a spotted sandpiper, a vagrant from North America. It was feeding along the muddy edges of one of the islands, seemingly oblivious to the frenetic screaming of hundreds of black-headed gulls, common and Sandwich terns and avocets. Marsh harriers glided over the reedbeds and two hobbies were catching dragonflies and eating them on the wing.

Minsmere from the air   *Photo:* Mike Page

Black-headed gulls at Minsmere   *Photo:* Rob Macklin

Spotted sandpiper at Minsmere   *Photo:* Terry McGeever

On to North Warren to carry out the weekly butterfly transect but very few on the wing after recent horrendous weather. I saw my first holly blue for a while and just one wall brown. The introduced tree lupin was coming into flower along the old railway track, being complemented by flowering spotted-medick, common vetch, bird's-foot trefoil, hop trefoil, germander speedwell and silverweed. The honey-scented tree lupin was introduced into Britain from California in 1793. It self-seeds readily in dry, frost-free areas and is widely naturalised on the Suffolk coast's sandy soils.

Still five avocets on the marshes and two lapwings furiously mobbed a passing marsh harrier.

Tree lupin on the old railway track   *Photo:* Rob Macklin

A lapwing mobbing a marsh harrier   *Photo:* Stuart Elsom

June
3rd - 10th
Eastern Hungary

In early June I accompanied the Salisbury Natural History Society to north-eastern Hungary with Honeyguide Wildlife Holidays. We were based in the small village of Nosvaj which was centrally placed to allow us to explore a range of wildlife habitats. The Bukk Hills are, in effect, foothills of the Carpathians and were established as a national park in 1976. The hills rise from 300m to 960m and habitats include mixed beech-hornbeam forests, oak-dotted pastures, rocky limestone slopes and flower-rich meadows. These habitats support nine species of woodpeckers including the magnificent black woodpecker and scarce white-backed woodpecker.

Valley in the Bukk Hills   *Photo:* Rob Macklin

The Hortobagy National Park is a UNESCO World Heritage Site comprising 80,000 hectares and is one of Europe's great wildlife areas. Approximately two thirds of the area is grassland and one third wetland areas, mostly large fishpond systems. The wetlands attract a whole host of specialist birds while the grasslands hold populations of great bustards and stone-curlews.

Fishponds at Hortobagy   *Photo:* Rob Macklin

4th

Bukk Hills National Park

A rather grey day with intermittent rain in the morning intensifying throughout the afternoon. Our first visit was to a superb small wetland area where river and great reed warblers were in full song, the latter perched up in the open, allowing excellent views. Several nightingales were also singing well and a male marsh harrier drifted past carrying prey.

Great reed warbler in full song   *Photo:* Stuart Elsom

Turtle doves and cuckoos appeared to be extremely widespread and abundant and four red-backed shrikes were perched up in open scrub on the hillside. It was extremely heartening to see such good numbers of turtle doves, cuckoos, shrikes and thrushes, all of which are in decline in the UK. Large numbers of the colossal Roman snails were out and enjoying the wet conditions. Dogwood was very common in the scrub at this site and whorled clary, birthwort and hemlock were all in flower.

Male red-backed shrike   ***Photo:*** Stuart Elsom

June
5th
Heves Grasslands & Lake Tisza

A woodland area near the village of Nosvaj was a known haunt of black woodpeckers and we were delighted to find an adult flying in to feed two young at the nest. A family of green woodpeckers were very active and noisy here and a great-spotted woodpecker called from deep within the wood.

Out on the open Heves grasslands two eastern imperial eagles were circling high overhead being mobbed by several lapwings; currently there are 75 pairs of these magnificent eagles breeding in Hungary. Elegant avocets and black-tailed godwits were feeding on flooded fields, lesser-grey shrikes seemed to be everywhere and small groups of tree sparrows and yellow wagtails were feeding on the track edges. A white stork's nest in a local village was occupied by one stork standing obligingly on the nest. There are now 5,000 pairs in Hungary.

We approached Lake Tisza in the afternoon along a bank with the lake on one side and an area of marshes on the other. Redshanks and lapwings were breeding on the marshes but the real highlight here was the abundance of grey, night and squacco herons! Like shafts of sunlight two golden orioles flew out of the scrub with a backdrop of singing reed buntings and great reed warblers; a male garganey appeared fitfully on open water on the marsh. Graceful great white egrets stalked fish in the shallows.

Out on the lake whiskered terns flew serenely over a group of great-crested grebes and mute swans before a striking male penduline tit perched up in the reeds in full view. A skulking warbler was tracked for several minutes before being identified as a barred warbler! Crown and yellow vetch were in full flower here.

A further visit to the open grasslands was rewarded by finding two magnificent saker falcons in and around a large nest box erected high on an electricity pylon.

Male large copper   *Photo:* Rob Macklin

Male penduline tit   *Photo:* Stuart Elsom

Both falcons were quite distant but not so a stunning red-footed falcon at its nest by the side of a relatively busy road. A flash of turquoise announced the presence of a flying roller and a passing black stork was mobbed furiously by two lapwings, almost certainly protecting chicks. Fire-bellied toads were calling loudly from the ditch systems and the first rays of sunshine persuaded a large copper butterfly on to the wing.

Bukk Hills National Park

Stunning – a male collared flycatcher   *Photo:* Stuart Elsom

A pair of spotted flycatchers had decided that the hotel in Nosvaj was the ideal place in which to build their nest. In the hotel gardens a stunning male collared flycatcher was hunting for insects amongst the trees.

Our first visit was to an old quarry in the Hor valley where early morning sunshine had tempted out several butterflies including orange-tip, silver-studded blue plus pearly and chestnut heath. The quarry sported some delightful plants with bloody cranesbill, peach-leaved bellflower, chicory, rock-rose and biting stonecrop providing a feast of colour. Walking farther along the country road we heard rock buntings calling and a raven *"cronked"* as it flew overhead. We climbed up to a high point finding richly-coloured dusky cranesbill, valerian, Nottingham catchfly and wild clary.

The group decided to have a picnic on the woodland edge overlooking a meadow full of scrub and flowering field scabious. Several butterflies were on the wing here and amongst the familiar green-veined whites, speckled woods and large skippers were at least three brightly-marked chequered skippers. Purple mullein, meadow clary and Solomon's seal were all in flower here but were overshadowed by a superbly colourful patch of the aptly-named sticky catchfly!

Delightful – bloody cranesbill, above, and sticky catchfly, right

Photos: Rob Macklin

Purple mullein, and
chequered skipper,
Photos: Rob Macklin

Late afternoon was blessed by sunny skies and warmer temperatures so we headed up to higher ground on the edge of the national park. More butterflies were on the wing including pale clouded yellow, stunning large coppers, common and silver-studded blues, brown argus and pearl-bordered fritillary. Four soaring birds of prey comprised the inevitable buzzards but the fourth turned out to be the only black kite seen during the week. The hillside here was awash with spectacular flowers, particularly tall pink, dropwort and the bizarre blue field eryngo.

June
7th

Another visit to a different area of the Bukk Hills, walking up a very quiet road through the forest accompanied by soaring buzzards and single goshawk and sparrowhawk. We encountered a superb meadow filled with a dazzling array of dusky cranesbill, peach-leaved bellflower, tall pink, mountain clover and meadow clary. Several extremely delicate wood white butterflies glided from flower to flower and a small elephant hawk-moth had attempted to hide away in a thick tussock of grass.

A superb meadow contained peach-leaved bellflower, above, and wood white butterfly, below   *Photos:* Rob Macklin

95

Continuing along the road and finding perennial honesty, sanicle and bastard balm on the way, we found our way barred as the road had been washed away by recent storms. Undeterred we decided to explore the lower part of the valley and were delighted to find several spikes of bird's-nest orchid under the many small-leaved limes and beeches. Toothwort was growing on the roadside with oxlip, yellow archangel and several types of helleborine. A flurry of activity in the surrounding forest finally revealed a family of very noisy white-backed woodpeckers, one of the rarest species to be found here. Just at that moment a female "rufous" form of cuckoo flashed into view and perched up in the trees overhead.

White-backed woodpecker   *Photo:* Stuart Elsom

Pearl-bordered fritillary   *Photo:* Rob Macklin

8th

Hortobagy National Park

An early start to the day for the long journey to the spectacular Hortobagy National Park. Our first stop was at a large sand martin colony overlooking a superb area of marshland. Large numbers of great white egrets feeding in the shallows were joined by several purple and night herons and a solitary little egret. Two bitterns boomed from dense cover and three spoonbills flew serenely past. The marshes were alive with whiskered, black and exquisite white-winged black terns all hawking for food over the marshes, hence their description as "marsh terns".

Wildfowl included occasional pochards, one ferruginous duck, greylag geese with chicks, three gadwall and a stunning male garganey.

Above, a plethora of wildlife –
white-winged black tern

Photo: Stuart Elsom

and right, a fire-bellied toad
in the hand

Photo: Rob Macklin

A very special bird here was the pygmy cormorant at one of its few sites in eastern Hungary; five perched up in a dead tree and were soon joined by five more. Black-tailed godwits probed the shallows while hundreds of sand martins continued to hawk for insects in company with several bee-eaters which also had hungry families back in the sand pit. This plethora of wildlife was rounded off by a stunning male red-footed falcon hunting over the nearby fields.

Hortobagy is well known for its many fish ponds, and the next visit was to a huge carp lake; our ears were immediately assaulted by the calls of edible frogs who were very active right on the edge of the lake. This was just one of a series of carp ponds and was teeming with ferruginous ducks amongst hundreds of pochards and coots. Spoonbills flew back and forth to one of their main breeding colonies estimated to hold at least 100 pairs of this spectacular bird! A series of *"pings"* announced the presence of bearded tits and several of these delightful birds moved through the reeds while a Savi's warbler *"reeled"* away in the background. Narrow-leaved everlasting pea and celery-leaved buttercup were in flower on the track around the lake and sharp eyes discovered fresh otter tracks. Fire-bellied toads were prolific here and we scooped one up to admire the strange markings on its belly!

We moved on to a series of smaller, more overgrown, ponds nearby. Another Savi's warbler was singing well from dense reed cover but this one finally came out into the open for all to see. Several night herons were perched up in full view but the real surprise here was a stunning male white-spotted bluethroat in full song at the back of the ponds! Both common and dwarf mallow were flowering along the path, joined by the impressive-looking henbane, flowering corncockle and water forget-me-not. To cap a splendid hour a marsh warbler sat in full view going through its whole repertoire of calls, mimicking as many as ten species!

Corncockle   *Photo:* Rob Macklin

Our final destination of the day was an area of open farmland in search of bustards! As we approached the area we encountered three more rollers and at least six red-footed falcons. We attempted to drive along farm tracks into the heart of the farmland but recent heavy rains had made them all but impassable! However an area of wet marsh hosted yet another booming bittern as well as spoonbills, lapwings and whiskered terns.

June

A lesser grey shrike was perched up in full view on a sodden hay bale and several brown smudges in the distance turned out to be a small group of five roe deer. Several buzzards were in the air but a much larger *"aquila"* raptor put up a whole field of terns and waders before being mobbed by several lapwings. Although never coming too close, with the aid of powerful telescopes we were able to identify a lesser spotted eagle!

A lesser grey shrike was perched in full view   *Photo:* Rob Macklin

A whiskered tern over flooded marshes   *Photo:* Rob Macklin

9th
Bukk Hills National Park

Our first expedition of the morning concentrated on local matters with a cursory exploration of Nosvaj. Walked up past a Duke of Argyll's tea plant sprouting out of the hedgerows where blackcaps were in full song and two white storks soared majestically overhead. Several tree sparrows had taken up residence in the local gardens, a black redstart sang from the house roofs and two ravens glided across the blue sky. It did not take long to find our quarry as two black and white Syrian woodpeckers moved swiftly through the village gardens calling as they went. A black and blue butterfly on the sun-drenched track turned out to be a new species, a chequered blue!

101

Chequered blue, left, and black-veined
whites, above
Photos: Rob Macklin

As the day was warming up we decided to re-visit the flower-filled meadow, only on this occasion concentrating on butterflies. Large coppers were fairly abundant but the star of the show was undoubtedly a stunning purple-shot copper! Green and sloe hairstreaks were easily disturbed from the surrounding scrub while several black-veined whites posed majestically on the swaying flower-heads. Yet another flock of bee-eaters, this one some thirty strong, appeared overhead, their fluty calls carrying far on the breeze. A visit to another nearby meadow produced several more fritillaries including an unexpected Nickerl's and a single Queen of Spain fritillary.

The last destination on this Hungarian foray took us into yet another superb remote valley. Butterflies were everywhere in the warm conditions, particularly chequered skipper, marsh and small pearl-bordered fritillary and the easily overlooked dingy skipper. On a large patch of wet mud many butterflies, particularly mazarine blues and grizzled skippers, were taking on essential minerals. Marsh fritillaries are particularly scarce in Britain but seemed to be everywhere in these fantastic meadows. Birds were less easily seen here although a honey buzzard soared overhead amongst several common buzzards. Two sturdy hawfinches took flight from the woodland edge and a lesser-spotted woodpecker quickly flew from tree to tree.

June

A local shepherd and his two dogs were keeping an eye on a herd of Hungarian grey cattle complete with a fierce-looking bull. These cattle have become scarce in recent years but are still used widely throughout the national park to graze the open pastures. Another sand pit was full of yet more bee-eaters and sand martins. We encountered a bee-keeper attempting to retrieve a swarm of bees by the many hives on the hillside.

A large dark butterfly on the outward track was finally identified as a woodland ringlet.

Butterflies were everywhere, including this marsh fritillary

Photo: Rob Macklin

Scarce breed – Hungarian grey cattle

Photo:
Rob Macklin

June 12th

Another fine, hot and sunny day on the Suffolk coast – the weather has taken a turn for the better in the last few days. Many more flowers are now coming out at River Hundred making a fine show, particularly common cat's-ear, cut-leaved cranesbill, prickly sow-thistle, foxglove, heath bedstraw and the deep purple flowers of marsh thistle. The first flowers of bell heather are just coming through. First black-tailed skimmer dragonflies on the wing.

White foxgloves at River Hundred   *Photo:* Rob Macklin

June

Yellow flag in the fen   *Photo:* Rob Macklin

15th

Looked for orchids in the fen this morning but could only find 14 flower spikes of southern marsh orchid. Colour was beginning to change the face of the fen with yellow rattle, ragged robin, yellow flag and common sorrel all in flower.

Two lizards were sunning themselves on the boardwalk as reed buntings sang weakly from the surrounding scrub and yellowhammers more stridently from the nearby heath. Brightly coloured cinnabar moths are now on the wing and they will be seeking out ragwort on which to deposit their eggs.

Left, southern marsh orchid –
abundant at North Warren.
Above, cinnabar moths are now
on the wing

Photos: Rob Macklin

Wild roses are in full flower on the heath and tree lupins are adding a splash of yellow; one or two viper's bugloss just coming out. Many red admirals and a few painted ladies were taking advantage of the warm sun at the Warren. Paid my first visit to the silver-studded blue butterfly colony on the Walks and found the first male butterfly on the wing.

Found another 24 flowering spikes of southern marsh orchids at the north end of the grazing marshes.

June 16th

Butterflies were few and far between today but I did find two brown argus on the open, sandy heath at the Warren. These delightful small butterflies were particularly scarce on the Suffolk coast until the 1990s when small colonies appeared all over the Sandlings. This appearance coincided with the advent of agricultural set-aside which allowed the butterfly's food plants, storksbill and dove's-foot cranesbill, to flourish, thereby aiding the insect's spread. A stunning bright-blue emperor dragonfly patrolling the dykes on South Marsh was the first sighting of the year. Even though all three avocet nests have failed five birds were still on South Marsh in good company with three little egrets. A stoat darted across the old railway track disappearing swiftly into the nettles.

Little egret in flight   *Photo:* Stuart Elsom

Later in the day I went up to Billeaford Hall. The old, decaying and deserted barns were home to nesting swallows while the surrounding scrub held singing yellowhammers, whitethroats, goldfinches and a family party of long-tailed tits. A passing sparrowhawk was mobbed by two jackdaws and a posse of smaller birds.

The old barns were home to nesting swallows   *Photo:* Rob Macklin

The hedge around the hall was thick and tall, made up of a tangle of plants including blackthorn, hawthorn, field maple, ash, wayfaring tree, dogwood, hornbeam and even Duke of Argyll's tea-plant! A member of the nightshade family *"Lycium barbarum"* is a scrambling shrub from Asia, grown as hedging and often naturalised in hedges and scrub close to human habitation. The plant is mildly poisonous to humans! Flowering dog-rose spilled out of the hedge, climbing white bryony tangled its way around the stems and the white flowers of bladder campion peeped out from the hedge-base.

Climbing white
bryony peers
through the hedge
Photo: Rob Macklin

108

The roadside between Knodishall and Aldringham was a real picture of flowering poppies, mallow and hedge parsley – alas, soon to fall victim to the council-sponsored verge-cutters!

Soon to fall victim of the council-sponsored verge-cutters – flowering mallow at Knodishall   *Photo:* Rob Macklin

June
17th

Encountered a beautiful cream-spot tiger moth at River Hundred. Fresh growth along the banks has transformed the Hundred river into a green paradise.

Green paradise – the Hundred River in mid-June.
Inset, a cream-spot tiger moth along the river   *Photos:* Rob Macklin

June 19th

Found a stunning male Dartford warbler amongst the gorse and heather on the Walks. He appeared to be carrying food so probably had a hungry brood hidden nearby. The colours on the male are truly astounding, particularly the dark wine-red of the underparts and glistening white spots on the throat. Several yellowhammers and goldcrests were singing joyously and a turtle dove "purred" from the edge of Square Covert.

I almost trod on a female adder on the narrow path through the heather before she quickly moved into cover. The disturbed ground along the main track through the Walks provides ideal conditions for creeping cinquefoil, red campion, common storksbill and houndstongue – the latter's flowers were described by 17th-Century herbalist John Pechey as a sordid red! The plant was prescribed in cases of dog-bite and occasionally worn in shoes to deter dogs!

A family party of six mistle thrushes called and scolded as they flew out of Margaret Wood.

I went out after dark looking for nightjars on the Walks. I found three churring males and just glimpsed the adults skimming low over the heath in pursuit of moths. Their old country name was "goatsucker" as farmers and shepherds believed they sucked milk from the teats of their livestock! A woodcock roded over Alexander Wood – a deep-throated growling sound followed by a high pitched squeak.

Found just one shining glow-worm!

"Goatsucker" is the old country name for nightjar

Photo: Graham Catley

June 22nd

Looked for wild flowers in the Haven fen, finding 82 flowering spikes of southern marsh orchid, narrow-leaved marsh orchid and early marsh orchid – there appeared to be some hybridisation too! Marsh thistle was very abundant and more colour was provided by ragged robin and bird's-foot trefoil. Adder's-tongue fern was scarcely visible amongst the fresh spring grass – closer inspection revealed a wealth of these small, scarce ferns in the grassland. These ferns were once in demand by herbalists and in the days of sympathetic magic were thought to be a cure for snake-bite!

Adder's-tongue fern at the Haven fen   *Photo:* John Davies

Over 100 pairs
of sedge
warblers
breed at
North Warren

Photo:
Mark Breaks

I found just three lilac spikes of flowering common broomrape growing amongst, and probably parasatising, hop trefoil. Swifts and swallows hawked for insects over the open fen while Cetti's, reed and sedge warblers were all singing their hearts out! A bullfinch sang softly from the banks of willows. My first large skipper of the year was taking advantage of the generous supply of nectar available from the marsh thistles.

I found just three
spikes of flowering
common broomrape

Photo: Rob Macklin

Passing through Snape I came across a set-aside field which was totally carpeted in blood-red poppies. This is the only field of poppies I have seen on the coast this year and they were growing with white campion, bugloss and field pansy while a splendid clump of musk thistle burst out of the nearby bank alongside sprawling black horehound, common mallow and mugwort.

A field at Snape was carpeted with blood-red poppies, above, while musk thistle burst out nearby

Photo: Rob Macklin

June
24th
Noar Hill, Selborne, Hampshire

Midsummer's Day. A very warm and sunny afternoon as we walked up through the Noar Hill Hangar, one of the woods made famous by Gilbert White and his "Natural History of Selborne".

A buzzard *"mewed"* overhead and blackcaps sang from the undergrowth in the wood. Enchanter's nightshade was in flower amongst wood spurge, hedge woundwort and woodruff. Various tracks through the wood were probably made by the local badgers.

On more open ground at the top of the wood we came across many flowering spikes of common spotted orchids. Dog's mercury and ramsons had now gone over but had been replaced by meadow vetchling and pendulous sedge. A marsh tit called from the depths of the wood.

We finally found the Noar Hill wildlife trust reserve and came across the first of many abandoned chalk pits which boasted an amazing array of calcareous plants. The area is known for its orchids and we were delighted to find carpets of fragrant orchids intermingled with pyramidal and common spotted orchids, a couple of late-flowering early purple orchids and just one twayblade! A wealth

Abandoned
chalk pit
at Noar Hill
Photo: Rob Macklin

of other chalk-loving plants included milkwort, salad burnet, carpets of sweet-smelling thyme and marjoram, hoary plantain, yellow rattle and large clumps of rock-rose.

The pit itself was surrounded by large mature beech trees interspersed with ash and field maples. A few butterflies put in an appearance, especially common blue, orange-tip and large skipper, then a chunky broad-bodied chaser dragonfly flew low across the clearing.

Fragrant orchid, left, and pyramidal orchid, right   *Photo:* Rob Macklin

116

June 29th

Sizewell village – home to swifts and house sparrows   *Photo:* Rob Macklin

Hot and sunny all day – it looks like summer is well and truly here at last. Sizewell village still retains a row of older cottages with tiled and slate roofs, providing excellent nesting sites for swifts and house sparrows, both of which were very active.

On the beach I found a superb clump of purple mallow against a creamy backdrop of delicate elder flowers. Several house martins had nests on the buildings at Cliff House and most seemed to have fledglings poking their heads out of the entrance holes. Honeysuckle, dog-roses and white bryony were spilling out of the scrub on the cliff top by Dower House. I came across a large flowering

Mallow and elder
in full flower at
Sizewell Beach
Photo: Rob Macklin

clump of musk, or knodding, thistle growing amongst poppies, weld, yarrow, storksbill and white campion at Ness House – a feast of early-summer colour. Common centaury was flowering on the open, dry and sandy grassland.

The road up to Home Farm is bordered on both sides by a thick, healthy hazel hedge, somewhat unusual on the Suffolk coast!

Hazel hedge on the road to Home Farm at Sizewell   *Photo:* Rob Macklin

Still very few butterflies on the wing, it seems to be the early summer gap between spring and summer flights. Reasonable numbers of meadow browns and small heaths were out at the Warren.

Both tufted and yellow vetchling are now in flower along the old railway track and the much-maligned ragwort is just coming out. A green form of the common lizard bolted across the boardwalk. A profusion of honeysuckle along the heath edge filled the air with perfume; on the dry grassland mallow, bugloss and viper's bugloss are in flower. The path across the marshes is lined by flowering dog and field roses. I found a small elephant hawk-moth pinned to the barbed wire on the livestock fence – perhaps a shrike in the area?

Honeysuckle in its full glory   *Photo:* Rob Macklin

Viper's bugloss on heath at North Warren   *Photo:* Rob Macklin

119

Above, flowering dog rose on the path across the marshes.
Below, small elephant hawk-moth impaled on barbed wire

Photos: Rob Macklin

June 30th

A three-foot long grass snake slithered across the road at Halfway Cottages near Sizewell. These reptiles have staged a remarkable recovery in recent years as they used to be extremely scarce here.

A deep, south-facing irrigation trench on the Walks was the site of an introduction of silver-studded blue butterflies several years ago by the RSPB. It was time for the first annual adult count of the year and after much backtracking and careful searching I came up with 108 stunningly bright males and just 25 dowdier females, still somewhat on the low side. The first small skipper was also found in this sheltered micro-climate while brown argus, small copper and small heath were all on the wing. A patrolling male emperor dragonfly did not appear to be targeting any of the butterflies.

Silver-studded blues at Aldringham Walks   *Photo:* Rob Macklin

Norfolk hawker dragonflies had been reported on the grazing marshes at the Warren so I searched the southern-most, reed-edged dykes on North Marsh. Several emperors and four-spotted chasers were patrolling the dykes while azure blue damselflies seemed to be ovipositing everywhere. I then had fantastic views of two Norfolk hawkers, one of Britain's most stunning and scarce dragonflies. They have been confined to the Norfolk Broads and it is unclear whether they have spread from there or are Continental immigrants – I think the latter might well be the case. This dragonfly is very similar to the brown hawker but can be easily recognised by its brown body, green eyes and clear, rather than brown, wings.

Norfolk hawker – one of Britain's most stunning and scarce dragonflies

Photo: Ian Barthorpe

The young Suffolk redpolls on the grazing marshes viewed me with evident suspicion as I made my way along the dyke edges   *Photo:* Rob Macklin

Still recovering from this marvellous experience I then surprised a bittern from the reedy shallows and it swiftly flew back towards the breeding area in the reedbed where at least two nests are still active. Another bittern, which could be recognised by its "dangly legs", then came up from under my feet, flying high into the air and towards the north end of the marshes.

Reed, sedge and Cetti's warblers were all still singing vigorously while the lapwings and redshanks continued to protect their young by driving off marauding crows and jackdaws. The marshes are now home to over 100 Suffolk redpoll cows and calves for the summer and the young ones viewed me with evident suspicion as I made my way along the dyke edges.

July is the seventh month of the year according to the
Gregorian calendar but was the fifth month in the early
calendar of the Romans, hence it was named Quintilius.
The Roman Senate renamed this month Julius in honour
of Julius Caesar, who was born on July 12th.

The Anglo-Saxons named July "Heymonath",
referring to haymaking time, or "Maed Monath" –
the flowering of hay meadows.

1st

Lady fern alongside the Hundred River   *Photo:* Rob Macklin

Hot and sunny again – a true taste of longed-for summer! Foxgloves are in full flower on the edge of the woods and the bright yellow flowers of tormentil are poking through the grass at River Hundred. A late green hairstreak fluttered around the gorse flowers.

Walked along the river to Skinny's bridge where several species of ferns were showing luxurious growth topped off by a splendid clump of lady fern on the water's edge. Hundreds of toadlets were on the boardwalk.

Went out on to Stonehouse Common after dark in search of glow-worms; I soon found several glowing females, which are unable to fly, crouching in the grass and signalling to any passing males that they are waiting for a partner. They are much less common than they used to be but can still be found in undisturbed corners of the Sandlings. Nightjars *"churred"* continuously on the open heath.

3rd

Another glorious summer's day with temperatures reaching 26°C in the shade! I carried out a one-hour watch from the high seat overlooking the reedbed this morning. Marsh harrier activity was intense with all three nesting females constantly in and around the reedbed, the lightly marked male overhead and two dark, freshly-fledged juveniles trying out their new-found freedom by flying strongly over the reed tops.

A female bittern flew out of the south-west corner of the reedbed towards the grazing marshes, intent on finding more food for her nestlings. A large male was seen twice in flight, *"cronking"* loudly as he flew low over the reeds to a new feeding area.

Bearded tits were busy gathering food for hungry broods and two males came unbelievably close to me, seemingly unaware of my presence. The blue-grey heads and the long, black drooping moustaches were very clear at such close quarters.

Two reed warblers were stripping the reedheads for nesting material to a backdrop of singing reed and Cetti's warblers, whitethroats, blackcaps and reed buntings. Male and female cuckoos were singing and bubbling from the scrub alongside the reeds and no doubt on the lookout for inviting reed warbler nests in which to deposit their eggs.

Several water rails squealed from the dense cover of the reeds and two hobbies sailed serenely overhead. It seemed as if the whole avian world was up to its neck in the business of nesting and raising families!

"If we had never before looked upon the Earth, but suddenly came to it man or woman grown, sat down in the midst of a summer mead, would it not seem to us a radiant vision? The hues, shapes, the song and life of birds, above all the sunlight, the breath of heaven, resting on it; the mind would be filled with its glory, unable to grasp it, hardly believing that such things could be mere matter and no more.

Like a dream of some spirit-land it would appear, scarce fit to be touched lest it should fall to pieces, too beautiful to be long watched lest it should fade away. So it seemed to me as a boy, sweet and new each morning; and even now, after the years that have passed, and the lines they have worn in the forehead, the summer mead shines as bright and fresh as when my foot first touched the grass."

**Richard Jeffries,
The Open Air**

Bittern in flight   *Photo:* Mark Breaks

126

Ragged robin flowering in the fen   *Photo:* Rob Macklin

As I walked back home through the dense vegetation I put up two very dainty emerald damselflies. Hemp agrimony and great hairy willow-herb are just coming into flower.

Still relatively few butterflies on the wing, notably an almost complete absence of the common whites; the green-veined white is the most abundant on the reserve and is not the "cabbage" white sometimes referred to; that distinction belongs to the large and small whites! Red admirals are plentiful this year and have now been joined by small numbers of painted ladies. Small heaths and ringlets are common at the moment and meadow browns are slowly becoming more numerous. The vegetation in the fen is becoming increasingly lush and, although mainly dominated by reed, good stands of yellow rattle and ragged robin are poking through the dead stems.

Woody nightshade is providing a burst of colour amongst the green willows. Otherwise known as "bittersweet" and often mis-identified as deadly nightshade, this plant is one of the less poisonous members of the family. The intense bitterness from which it derives its name causes most curious nibblers to spit out the berries immediately.

Bittersweet or woody nightshade   *Photo:* Rob Macklin

More colour is now coming into the hedgerows and along the old railway track, the yellows, pinks and whites of lady's bedstraw, yellow vetchling, tutfted vetch, yarrow, bird's-foot trefoil, weld, nipplewort, common storksbill and the aptly named perforate St. John's wort whose translucent dots on the leaves look like tiny holes against the light.

128

Lady's bedstraw
is common across
the reserve
Photo: Rob Macklin

Lady's bedstraw is particularly common across the reserve but its use by country folk has long since vanished. The most common use of this plant was as a form of rennet to curdle milk when making cheese, giving it the country name of cheese-rennet. In Gloucestershire it was mixed with nettle juice to make Double Gloucester. The flowering tops, distilled with water, yield an acid liquor which is said to form a pleasant summer drink.

A pair of cuckoos flew over the heath calling and bubbling.

Cuckoo   *Photo:* Mark Breaks

Heavy rain first thing, giving way to a bright and sunny morning. I headed south to Sudbourne to take a look at the recently purchased Suffolk Wildlife Trust reserve at Captain's Wood. A thick hedge along the entrance track was dominated by field maple on one side and hazel on the other. Crossing an area of open grassland I saw one dark and one very light fallow deer while both great-spotted and green woodpeckers were noisily active in the woods. This grassland area was arable land up to the 1990s but is now slowly reverting back to acid grassland and wood pasture. Colonising flowering plants included hop trefoil, self heal, white clover, bird's-foot trefoil, ragwort, creeping thistle, white campion and the striking common centaury.

Common centaury at Captain's Wood, Sudbourne   *Photo:* Rob Macklin

On the marshes themselves I encountered a suckler herd complete with a large, fierce-looking, black bull – fortunately he was on the other side of the dyke! Walking along a reed-fringed dyke with the inevitable reed warblers in song I found water plantain in flower. An oystercatcher flew straight at me piping loudly, a sure indication that it was protecting its young. A grey heron stood sentinel-like on the edge of a reedy dyke and a pair of coots ushered their young into the cover of the dense reeds.

A female emperor dragonfly was egg-laying on water weeds in the dyke, a late hairy dragonfly was still on the wing and several four-spotted chasers buzzed back and forth over the open water of the borrow dyke (so called because the excavated material was used to build the sea wall, hence "borrowed"). A mute swan stood on a flattened empty nest, probably with her cygnets nearby, and the first gatekeeper of the year fluttered along the hedgerow as I made my way back to Sudbourne.

Left, a grey heron stood sentinel.
Photo: John Archibald

Below, great hairy willow-herb on
Sudbourne Marshes
Photo: Rob Macklin

For many species the breeding season is now over – especially for a number of wading birds. These are beginning to pass through the reserve and the muddy, shallow edges of south marsh had attracted 35 black-tailed godwits, three avocets and two green sandpipers. A pair of mute swans have turned up in the central marsh dyke with four large cygnets.

Several emperor and four-spotted chaser dragonflies were very active along the open dykes, black-tailed skimmers were everywhere and I found my first ruddy darter of the year. In one of the fields pignut and celery-leaved buttercup were in flower although most of the ground was carpeted in bird's-foot trefoil and bulbous buttercup. A bank of bright yellow goatsbeard looked stunning against a backdrop of rushes and reeds. The cattle have yet to graze these fields so the plants have a chance to set seed; a nearby Charolais bull cast envious eyes over the verdant vegetation.

Charolais bull with cattle on South Marsh   *Photo:* Rob Macklin

Children from Snape school were engrossed on a visit to Priory Wood
Photo: Rob Macklin

In the afternoon, children of Snape primary school visited the new community woodland, Priory Wood. They spent an engrossing two hours looking at plants and insects but were particularly enthralled by two great green bush crickets. Brown argus and large skipper butterflies were also in flight.

Later in the afternoon I made my way through the head-high nettles in Little Beauties Wood to find the areas of surviving wych elm.

The only surviving
mature wych elm on
Aldringham Walks
Photo: Rob Macklin

137

I was delighted to find five white-letter hairstreak butterflies buzzing around the coppiced regrowth; this is one of the hardest butterflies to find in Suffolk. Stunningly fresh and bright commas were also on the wing, taking the abundant nectar from the massed banks of brambles.

White-letter hairstreak is one of the hardest butterflies to find

Photo:
Richard Thomas

12th

Still sunny and hot although an onshore breeze brought some relief. Meadowsweet is now in full flower in the fen and several purple loosestrife flower spikes are also coming through. The whole area is a tangle of flowering greater bird's-foot trefoil, marsh thistle and tufted vetch. The introduced Himalayan balsam seems to be continuing its inexorable march along the banks of the Hundred river, even making progress through the dense nettle beds. It was introduced to British gardens from the Himalayas in 1839 and had become widely naturalised by the end of the nineteenth century. It has

July 13th

A visit to Abbey Farm in Snape this morning where skylarks were still in song and reed warblers called from reed-fringed dykes. Three grey herons flapped lazily by whereas a turtle dove flew low over the marshes at great speed. The edges of the higher arable fields were full of flowers, particularly the bright yellow common fleabane, fumitory, mallow, scentless mayweed and both creeping and spear thistles. Still a few banded demoiselles on the Fromus river where flower spikes of yellow water-lily were pushing up through the water. Lots of common cudweed and hare's-foot clover found near the farmhouse.

Common fleabane at Abbey Farm   *Photo:* Rob Macklin

July 15th

S t. Swithin's Day. St. Swithin was a Saxon bishop of Winchester who asked to be buried out of doors where he would be trodden and rained on. Hot and sunny with a light onshore breeze.

St. Swithin's Day, if thou dost rain,
For forty days it will remain.
St. Swithin's Day, if thou be fair,
For forty days 'twill rain nae mair.

16th

W ent up to Dunwich Forest this morning to search for white admiral butterflies; I did not have to go far into the wood before I found three of the impressive butterflies nectaring on bramble flowers in a clearing. White admirals have spread in recent years on the Suffolk coast and can now be found at Minsmere, Dunwich and Theberton Wood.

Privet is in flower at Aldringham Church and has attracted hordes of bees and butterflies including both Essex and small skippers, painted ladies, gatekeepers and especially small tortoiseshells which are generally very scarce at the moment.

Painted lady
on privet at
Aldringham Church
Photo: Rob Macklin

Sea pea, left, yellow-horned poppy, right, and, below, sea kale, all on Aldeburgh beach

Photos: Rob Macklin

The intense heat has all but dried up the vegetation on the heath and the beach although I was still able to find flowering plants on the shingle ridge. Both sea pea and yellow-horned poppy were in full bloom while great clumps of sea kale have appeared all along the ridge; the latter has increased enormously in recent years.

143

Sea holly was just coming into flower on the grass by Haven House and there were still carpets of bright yellow lady's bedstraw and pink common restharrow. Both grayling and small coppers were taking nectar from the flowers and a bright male common blue was the first of the second generation. Several silver Y moths on the wing.

Sea holly at Thorpeness   *Photo:* Rob Macklin

18th

Even hotter today with cloudless skies and a gentle onshore breeze. I came across a line of chicory in flower along the country lanes at Theberton. The unblanched leaves of wild chicory are bitter, but tolerable in a mixed salad; the dried and ground roots have long been used as an additive, and sometimes substitute, for coffee.

Both brown and southern hawkers were on the wing at River Hundred and later in the afternoon I was able to find three purple hairstreak butterflies fluttering around the crowns of the mature oak trees. Harvesting is now well under way on the Suffolk coast.

Chicory at Theberton   *Photo:* Rob Macklin

20th

Exmoor

We stayed overnight in the small hamlet of Loxhore Cott, with tawny owls calling throughout the night and the dawn chorus dominated by a single song thrush. Surprisingly grey and cool as we walked to Heddon's Mouth along the river from the Hunter's Inn. Walking through sessile oak woods the ground flora was dominated by male fern and Hart's-tongue fern with enchanter's nightshade filling in the gaps.

145

Leaving the woods we made our way through bracken-covered hillsides interspersed with shale scree, ling, bell heather and wood sage. Several bright-orange silver-washed fritillaries were taking nectar from bramble and brown knapweed flowers and were joined by two much rarer high-brown fritillaries which made occasional lightning-fast sorties onto the bramble flowers from the high slopes above.

Silver-washed fritillary on brown knapweed   *Photo:* Rob Macklin

Approaching the sea we encountered buck's-horn plantain, bright blue sheep's-bit and a few remaining thrift flowers. A family of kestrels were very active along the high ridge and a passing buzzard was quickly seen off by nesting herring gulls who were protecting large, almost fledged youngsters. Two large, brooding, great black-backed gulls stood stock-still on the rocks while a fulmar glided by on very stiff wings.

Rocky river above Heddon's Mouth – a haunt of dippers   *Photo:* Rob Macklin

We investigated a well-restored lime kiln which was chock-full of rusty-back fern. Hemlock water-dropwort and valerian were growing along the river and we had superb views of both dipper and grey wagtail on the rocks in the fast-flowing water. As the dipper blinked the membrane across the eye, which allows it to hunt underwater, became very obvious. Ringlet butterflies were very common here but, in these more sheltered conditions, much fresher than their east Suffolk cousins.

We walked down to Tarr Steps, a medieval stone bridge over the River Barle. The meadow above the river was full of flowering yarrow and brown knapweed attracting a wide range of common butterflies but also one or two marbled whites (a species which is actually a "brown").

147

In the afternoon we stopped on Exmoor between Simonsbath and Dulverton at Winsford Hill. We found all three of the commoner heathers in flower including the paler cross-leaved heath. The moor itself was tinder-dry but still supported flowering lousewort, tormentil and common cow-wheat while bilberry was extremely abundant. A hobby flashed low over the moor.

21st
Somerset

An afternoon at Otterhead Lakes – two large ones, although there were originally seven. The margins were absolutely heaving with common blue damselflies interspersed with occasional keeled skimmer and emperor dragonflies.

Otterhead Lakes in Somerset   *Photo:* Rob Macklin

Male brimstone on sunflowers   *Photo:* Rob Macklin

Orange balsam was growing alongside one of the canals and two patches of sunflowers had attracted scores of freshly emerged peacocks plus several painted ladies, small tortoiseshells and red admirals. The scene was further enlivened by a single, bright yellow, male brimstone, several marbled whites and many fresh commas – a truly magnificent sight. Flowering betony and greater knapweed completed the picture.

23rd

The hottest day of the year so far on the Suffolk coast with temperatures up to 27°C and a light south-easterly breeze. A superb day for butterflies with new-generation peacocks, brown argus and common blues on the wing together with encouraging numbers of graylings, gatekeepers and Essex skippers. The ringlets are beginning to look faded and meadow brown numbers are on the wane. Several painted ladies and commas look amazingly fresh!

Dragonflies are beginning to become more obvious with excellent numbers of ruddy darters in flight, the local population probably supplemented by continental immigrants. Several brown and southern hawkers were joined by the first migrant hawkers – as their name suggests, in some years many thousands will find their way to the UK from the near Continent. Hoverflies are everywhere!

Migrant hawker, a visitor from the near Continent   *Photo:* Rob Macklin

On the old railway track the bright yellow flowers of tansy have been joined by flowering wild parsnip. In the fen, meadowsweet seems to have taken over while purple loosestrife is also providing a splash of colour. On the heath edge I found a magnificent clump of great mullein, one flower spike sporting a huge great green bush cricket. Harebells are out.

Small red-eyed damselfly   *Photo:* Richard Thomas

25th

Continuing hot and sunny and an ideal time to look in depth at the dragonflies on South Marsh. Eleven species were found including 278 adults of the small red-eyed damselfly, the most recent colonist from mainland Europe. This dainty damselfly actively seeks out more open water in the dyke system and has benefited from mechanical rotational clearing of the vegetation in the dykes. Common blue damselflies and ruddy darters were also out in good numbers and I counted at least 100 black-tailed skimmers, the males resplendent with their powder-blue abdomens "dipped in ink". The top dog, the emperor dragonfly, patrolled the open dykes and several females were egg-laying into the water from the floating vegetation.

Strawberry clover and red bartsia are now out in flower across the grazing marshes plus huge amounts of the very invasive sea-club rush. The gull roost on South Marsh included two striking little gulls in summer plumage and four green sandpipers were feeding on the muddy edges on their way back south.

Little gulls in summer plumage   *Photo:* Stuart Elsom

28th

L ooked for dragonflies on North Marsh today – excellent numbers of ruddy darters, emperors on any stretch of open water and small red-eyed damselflies abundant. Perhaps the find of the day were four extremely dainty emerald damselflies, hard to pick out amongst the emergent vegetation.

Frogbit in dykes at North Warren   *Photo:* Rob Macklin

Flowering great hairy willow-herb has attracted a wide range of hungry insects while in the dykes frogbit has responded well to clearance work and is a mass of pure white flowers.

Gypsywort, water mint and common fleabane in flower along the dyke edges and water plantain has just started to come out. Several fresh painted ladies are on the wing. Flushed yet another bittern from the reedy dyke edges and this one flew back towards the reedbed *"cronking"* loudly. A flock of 21 curlews rose from the marshes uttering their very characteristic bubbling calls.

153

July 30th

S cores of gatekeeper butterflies were taking nectar from the flowering bell heather on the heath. Two purple hairstreak butterflies occasionally took to the wing around the crowns of the oak trees in the intense heat. Swifts are still wheeling overhead.

Bell heather at Aldringham Walks   *Photo:* Rob Macklin

31st

T he heatwave is over for now as squally showers sweep in from the north-west bringing an early taste of autumn to mid-summer; yesterday's butterflies are nowhere to be seen.

MAURICE HARVEY

Bitter Sweet - woody night shade

Lammas Day - (Leaf Moss

Lifeboats

The purchase of this item contributes to the
lifesaving work of the Royal National Lifeboat Institution

SAVING LIVES SINCE 1824

RNLI (SALES) LTD · POOLE · DORSET · Tel 01202 663000
www.lifeboats.org.uk
REGISTERED CHARITY NO. 209603

August

*August was the sixth month of the Roman calendar
and was named Sextilis. In 8BC the month
was changed to Augustus in
honour of the Emperor Augustus Caesar.*

*Th Anglo-Saxons called August "Weod Monath"
as it was the period when weeds and other plants
were most plentiful.*

1st

Lammas Day! The name derives from the Anglo-Saxon "Hlafmaesse" which means Loaf Mass. The festival of Lammas marks the beginning of the harvest and thanks were given for its safe delivery. Oak trees put on a spurt of leaf growth at this time, hence the name "lammas growth".

2nd

Cool and breezy with showers. A heavy crop of mast on the stately beech trees at River Hundred will provide a welcome bounty for over-wintering bramblings and chaffinches.

Beechmast at
River Hundred
Photo: Rob Macklin

Several sandwich and common terns were in the gull roost on South Marsh; 17 black-tailed godwits were feeding in the shallows.

Common tern in flight   *Photo:* Stuart Elsom

5th

The swifts have now all but departed for Africa but another summer stalwart, a turtle dove, was *"purring"* from the thickets at River Hundred. Another superb day for butterflies with many fresh painted ladies and red admirals on the wing and it has been one of the best seasons in recent years for the scarce grayling. Two brown argus and a small copper were feeding together on tansy flowers, somewhat surprising as this plant is usually avoided by most insects. Hundreds of silver Y moths added to the mix. Several bright southern hawkers continued to patrol the open spaces of the paths and tracks.

Small copper and brown argus on tansy   *Photo:* Rob Macklin

Angelica is flowering in the fen, providing a rich tapestry of colour with greater bird's-foot trefoil, hemp agrimony, purple loosestrife, gypsywort, marsh thistle and particularly meadowsweet.

The latter, together with water-mint and vervain, were the three herbs held most sacred by the Druids. Often associated with death, it is considered unlucky to bring it into the house. It is said that the scent can induce a deep sleep from which the sleeper may not wake! Even so, meadowsweet was a common strewing herb, used to cover the floors of houses before carpets became commonplace, to impart a pleasant smell to the rooms. In medieval times the flowers were used to flavour mead and also used as a substitute when honey was in short supply because of their similar flavour.

The old railway track was bursting with flowering wild parsnip, weld, yarrow, brown knapweed and a patch of shocking-pink broad-leaved everlasting pea. The first blackberries are fruiting and the blackthorns are laden with unripe sloes.

157

Purple loosestrife and angelica in the fen   *Photo:* Rob Macklin

Broad-leaved everlasting pea on the railway track
Photo: Rob Macklin

158

August
8th

Rowan berries are very much in evidence at River Hundred and will provide essential food for our resident thrushes. The berries are also fit for humans and with a few crab apples make a sharp, "marmaladish" jelly. The juice of freshly squeezed rowan berries can also be added to gin in place of angostura bitters!

Rowan berries are very much in evidence at River Hundred

Photo: Rob Macklin

Found a large emerald moth perched out in the open in full sun along the old railway track. Painted ladies were taking nectar from creeping thistle.

Still 20 black-tailed godwits feeding in the shallows on South Marsh.

Large emerald moth

Photo: Rob Macklin

159

August
10th

The Haven fen is a kaleidoscope of colour dominated by hemp agrimony, the yellows of common fleabane and ragwort, plus dense flowering banks of the introduced Japanese rose, *"Rosa rugosa"*. Pignut, tufted vetch, centaury, water mint and angelica completed an astounding picture. Scores of common blue butterflies were feeding on the flowers with a few painted ladies. A sparrowhawk flashed past, no doubt intent on its own business! Several stunted apple trees, probably introduced here via seed from birds, are laden with fruit.

Several stunted apple trees are laden with fruit   *Photo:* Rob Macklin

Harebells – scarce in 2006   *Photo:* Rob Macklin

Very few harebells out, just odd ones on Thorpeness Common. The first of the second generation of holly blue butterflies were out at River Hundred.

Eight cormorants roosting on the mud banks were joined by 33 feeding black-tailed godwits and two redshanks.

12th

Torrential rain all day and by far the wettest day of the year on a cold northerly wind. An otter, delighting in the wet conditions danced through the grassy heath at River Hundred.

August
13th

Walberswick was extremely busy due to the annual "crabbing" championship so I left the crowds behind and took the opportunity to walk up the south side of the Blyth estuary. Passing Robinson's Marshes I came across a herd of 30 heifers overwhelmed by a sea of grass on Tinker's Marsh. Several whimbrel flew up as the cattle continued to feed and a greenshank called as it flew down river. The river walls are protected by reasonable-quality saltmarsh dominated by sea purslane and the more colourful sea lavender. Dense sea couch grass clothed the river walls

I found a dead redshank on the towpath.

Sea lavender on the saltmarsh at Walberswick   *Photo:* Rob Macklin

16th

Ripening sloes are dripping off the bushes along the old railway track. The colour on show in the fen is astounding and the striking purple loosestrife is putting on its most impressive show of flowers for many years. Gypsywort, angelica and fleabane all added to the mix.

Coal tits are beginning to sing again! Bracken clearing has begun on the Warren. Migrant hawkers are very abundant at the moment, numbers certainly swelled by immigrants from the Continent. I came across a five-foot-high great mullein plant on the heath edge.

162

I came across a five-foot great mullein on the edge of the heath
Photo: Rob Macklin

Fennel is in flower on the beach – easily identified by its distinctive pungent aroma. Fennel never looks convincingly native on Suffolk waysides, its hair-like plumes of bright green leaves seem exotic by the side of rustic native relatives such as hogweed. It was probably introduced by the Romans as a medicinal and culinary herb. The leaves smell strongly of aniseed and are widely used in cooking – a sauce of chopped fennel and gooseberry is a classic accompaniment to oily fish such as mackerel.

163

August
17th

Small parties of swallows were flying south along the beach this morning. The Haven fen is alive with common blue butterflies. Toadflax very abundant on the drier ground.

A brood of sparrowhawks called noisily in the birch woods at River Hundred.

18th

A stunning Camberwell beauty was on the buddleia bushes at Minsmere accompanied by red admirals and painted ladies. This rare and enchanting butterfly occasionally turns up on the Suffolk coast in late summer, an immigrant from continental Europe.

A stunning Camberwell beauty was on the buddleia bushes at Minsmere

Photo: Rob Macklin

August

19th

A sparrowhawk was being mobbed by several house martins over Margaret Wood. Seven red admirals in the garden at River Hundred were feeding avidly on a profusion of "hebe" flowers.

21st

The heath at Aldringham Walks looks an absolute picture, swathed in purple heather and bright yellow western gorse flowers. Scores of swallows were taking insects on the wing over the heath. A terrific thunderstorm in early afternoon – and on Aldeburgh Carnival day!

Heather and western gorse at Aldringham Walks   *Photo:* Rob Macklin

August 22nd

Butterfly numbers are starting to decline although good numbers of speckled woods today, largely feeding on ripe blackberries while green-veined whites were concentrating on brown knapweed flowers. A very bright comma feeding on angelica in the fen was the first of the autumn generation.

Flowering plants are also in decline but a few late-summer blooms included creeping thistle, black horehound, common mallow, brown knapweed, red bartsia, tansy, yarrow, upright hedge-parsley, hemp agrimony, St. John's wort, field bindweed and ragwort. Wasp galls, known as robin's pincushion, are forming on the rose bushes on the banks of the marshes. Three kestrels were hunting over the marshes, probably for voles, but also keen to take the larger bush crickets.

Robin's pincushion   *Photo:* Rob Macklin

**Kingfisher at Darsham Marshes
and, inset, water mint**

Main photo: Stuart Elsom
Inset photo: Rob Mackin

A cool grey afternoon found me at Darsham Marshes, a Suffolk Wildlife Trust reserve, on the Minsmere River between Westleton and Yoxford. The vegetation here is dominated by pond sedge although the cattle seemed to be making inroads into it. The white flowers of common hemp-nettle intermingled with the purple flowers of water mint while the hawthorns on the drier ground were dripping with berries.

Three grey herons took flight and a brilliant blue kingfisher flashed away along a recently cleared dyke. A female and young male red deer melted away into the scrub. One particular section of the marsh was carpeted in angelica, water mint and marsh thistle with patches of greater bird's-foot trefoil, meadowsweet, gypsywort and great hairy willow-herb.

A great many alders have invaded the wetter areas of the marsh and some of these are dying back. Came across a dyke choked with reedmace towering over sheets of water forget-me-not.

Water forget-me-not   *Photo:* Rob Macklin

At the north end of the marsh I investigated a disused crag pit full of gorse, some of which had been "topiarised" by rabbits, and heavily grazed acid grassland. Found a puffball, *"Calvatia utriformis"* – this is the largest puffball after the giant puffball and can be as much as six inches high.

Puffball – *Calvatia utriformis*   Photo: Rob Macklin

Torrential rain overnight continued periodically throughout the day. The roads were flooded at Aldringham and Snape. A flock of 160 house martins were feeding over the marshes and my first whinchat of the autumn was on the central bank.

Huge parasol mushrooms now out at River Hundred and on the higher ground on the edge of the marshes. This fairly common mushroom normally stands well above the surrounding grass and is easily found. A single parasol is enough for one person and they are excellent fried in batter and served with courgettes or broccoli!

Parasol at River Hundred   *Photo:* Rob Macklin

25th

S unny and warm all day – a blessed relief! A good day for birds of prey crowned by an osprey drifting slowly south, heading for warmer, winter climes. A sparrowhawk soared over Aldeburgh Church while a pair of marsh harriers and two kestrels were hunting over the marshes.

Yesterday's heavy rain has brought in more teal with at least 86 now on South Marsh. Three grey herons and three little egrets were hunting along the dyke edges. Whinchat numbers were up to four on the beach, 12 swifts were high overhead at River Hundred and 280 house martins hawked for insects over the marshes.

A large clump of hemp agrimony amongst the beach scrub had attracted large numbers of common blue butterflies plus odd graylings, brown argus and painted ladies.

Grayling on hemp agrimony   *Photo:* Rob Macklin

26th

Three hobbies were hawking for insects over the heath; one flashed away high into the sky to make an unsuccessful dart at a passing swift. Hobbies are the only bird of prey capable of taking swifts in flight.

Swift

Photo: Mark Breaks

27th

A honey buzzard drifted slowly south across the sky and a female marsh harrier was quartering the reedbed. Several more migrants on the marshes included three whinchats, two yellow wagtails, a pied flycatcher and 30 black-tailed godwits.

Black-tailed godwit   *Photo:* Stuart Elsom

28th

T he first small tortoiseshells since July 15th were at River Hundred and Sizewell Common. This usually common butterfly has declined markedly in recent years on the Suffolk coast; it is possible that they are suffering from the spread of the parasite Tachinid fly *"Sturmia bella"*.

172

August
31st

Robins are singing again at River Hundred. Went blackberrying around North Marsh – a fair crop but very few elderberries. Perhaps the birds have beaten me to it!

"A generation ago, blackberry-picking time was an event on the calendar almost as significant as that of Christmas or Easter. Whole families from town and city, armed with buckets and 'tilly' cans, descended on the countryside and plundered the roadsides, hedges, woods and wasteground. There is a taboo against eating black-berries after October 10th because, during that night, the Devil goes by and spits on every bush. In fact, the fruit does tend to become watery and flavourless after night frosts although autumn frosts are now something of a rarity on the Suffolk coast."

Blackberries have a wealth of uses including wine-making, syrup, jams and pies but perhaps a lesser known use is for "Blackberry Ale".

"Is composed of strong wort made from two bushels of malt and a quarter pound of hops. To this is added the juice of a peck of ripe blackberries and a little yeast. After fermentation the cask was stopped up close for six weeks, the ale was then bottled, and was fit to drink at the end of another fortnight."

**The Curiosities of Ale & Beer,
John Bickerdyke, 1886**

**Blackerries at
North Warren**
Photo: Rob Macklin

September

September derives from the Roman word "septem" as it was the seventh month in the Roman calendar. The Romans believed it was sacred to the god Vulcan. As the god of fire and forge they expected September to be associated with fires, earthquakes and volcanic eruptions.

The Anglo-Saxons called it "Gerst Monath" (Barley month) as the harvested barley was made into "barley-brew". It was also named "Haefest Monath" or Harvest month.

1st

Heavy overnight rain but sunny and reasonably warm all day. The open water at the east end of the reedbed was covered in a mass of yellow flowers of greater bladderwort. Many of the alders at the back of Thorpe Meare are dying due to *"Phytophthora"*, a fungal infection, although a good number of healthy ones remain.

Hart's-tongue fern was glowing green on the bridge at Three Arches, its only site in the area. A bright blue male black-tailed skimmer dragonfly flew low over the marshes – probably the last one of the year.

Hart's-tongue fern at Three Arches bridge

Photo: Rob Macklin

174

Mute swans on Thorpe Meare   *Photo:* Rob Macklin

Mute swan numbers on the Meare have reached a summer peak of 71 birds, all happily accepting handouts from visitors.

4th

Collected many ceps from the birch woods at River Hundred; they have become difficult to find here in recent years and although these were past their best they would still make for a tasty supper.

Ceps fit for an
autumn feast
Photo: Rob Macklin

September
5th

Occasional sunny periods and extremely warm for early September at 24°C with a light westerly breeze. Several migrants were on the edge of the marshes, including three yellow wagtails, two wheatears, two common whitethroats and a lesser whitethroat. A group of 18 black-tailed godwits were feeding in the shallows on South Marsh while the ringed plover high-tide roost on the beach held 63 birds. Several woodpigeons were making short work of ripe elderberries in the beach scrub.

Woodpigeon   *Photo:* Stuart Elsom

Two marsh harriers and three kestrels were hunting and soaring over North Marsh. Butterflies were enjoying the warm conditions with good numbers of speckled woods on the wing joined by two holly blues and two late graylings. Funghi were beginning to poke through, including a group of field mushrooms on the grassy part of the beach and a splendid blusher in the woods at the Warren. Dogwood berries on the old railway track gave an autumn flavour and fruits were forming on the sweet chestnut trees at Maplestead Farm.

A splendid blusher was in the woods at North Warren   *Photo:* Rob Macklin

Dogwood berries along the old railway track   *Photo:* Rob Macklin

Several clumps of harebells were in flower on the heath edge and three common lizards were encountered on the boardwalk. Ripe elderberries very much in evidence now while acorns and wasp galls are beginning to form on the oaks.

Elderberries have long been thought to have therapeutic powers and if gathered on St. John's Eve were traditionally thought to protect the possessor against witchcraft and also to bestow magical powers. The Romans used the juice of the berries as a hair dye and sometimes the dried berries can be used as a substitute for raisins. Elderberry cordial has long been used for colds and coughs and has recently been scientifically proved to be effective. Elderberries contain viburnic acid which induces perspiration and is especially useful in cases of bronchitis. Elderberry wine has always enjoyed a good reputation and was once so popular that whole orchards of elders were planted in Kent and the berries sold for wine-making.

Elderberry Wine
1lb elderberries
Pectin enzyme
Wine yeast
2 Campden tablets
2.2lb sugar

Crush the berries thoroughly in a strong polythene bag to break the skins. Add two pints boiling water and campden tablets and leave overnight in a covered container. Next day, add four pints warm water, pectin and activated wine yeast. Put in a gallon jar, fit airlock and leave for three days. Colour will return to normal at this stage. Strain through jelly bag or muslin and return to clean jar. Insert airlock and leave in a warm place to ferment out – approximately six weeks. Syphon off sediment into clean jar and leave to clear. Repeat this process if necessary. Bottle and store in a cool place.

At dusk a hobby drifted low over the house towards the reedbed, two tawny owls called in the woods at River Hundred and several pipistrelle bats swarmed around the house.

Ripe elderberries and, inset,
acorns and wasp galls

Photos: Rob Macklin

9th

Duck numbers are now building up on the marshes with 140 teal but just six shoveler there this morning. A Cetti's warbler sang briefly from the reedbed edge and a hobby was hawking for dragonflies along the dykes on South Marsh.

**Clouded yellow below
Thorpeness Cliffs**
Photo: John Davies

The female red-footed falcon that thrilled visitors
at Minsmere   *Photo:* Adam Rowlands

   At nearby Minsmere a female red-footed falcon continued to thrill numerous
visitors. A rare visitor from eastern Europe, recent years have brought an
upsurge in occurrences along the Suffolk coast. A flock of 25 goldfinches, aptly
named a "charm", were feeding on thistleheads on the marshes and a clouded
yellow was found on the beach below Thorpeness Cliffs.

180

September 10th

A glorious September day with temperatures rising to 23°C and just a light onshore breeze. An excellent day for small heath butterflies on the Warren, including 46 in just one small area. Still several small coppers flying plus both brown and southern hawker dragonflies; the latter can be very inquisitive and will fly up to inspect any walkers, who need not worry as they are completely harmless.

A grass snake, which must have been over two feet long, slithered towards me on the heath before making off through the dense bracken. Robins are now singing in earnest, setting up their winter territories, while both chiffchaffs and willow warblers were tempted into song before undertaking their long journeys south.

15th

Four whinchats and two wheatears on the beach were the only southbound migrants found today. I came across a dead young male sparrowhawk at the Haven fen. A peacock butterfly and several small coppers were feeding on the bright yellow flowers of common fleabane. A convolvulous hawk-moth was reported on Sizewell Common.

Convolvulous
hawk-moth
Photo: Robin Harvey

16th

Early autumnal mist evaporated to reveal a sunny and warm day with a light northerly breeze. A large dead hedgehog was on the road by River Hundred; they have been very scarce again this year. Fox dung here was full of blackberries. Dragonflies still abound with substantial numbers of migrant hawkers and common darters flying, though most ruddy darters have now disappeared. A very late brown argus butterfly was on the wing along the old railway track.

The evocative calls of curlews echoed across the marshes and teal numbers had reached over 200 birds. Still many plants in flower including white dead-nettle, common stork's-bill, viper's bugloss and climbing white-bryony.

Teal in flight
Photo: Stuart Elsom

17th

Time for the first national wildfowl count of the new season! Duck numbers were low although teal numbers had risen to 260 and 90 ringed plovers on the beach were coping with disturbance by walkers and bathers.

Two immature pectoral sandpipers on South Marsh were a real highlight, wandering migrants from America who just might find their way back home! Very few other migrants about but two swallows were heading south to warmer climes.

Pectoral sandpiper: a rare visitor from North America   *Photo:* Mark Breaks

I came across a storm-lashed elder tree on North Marsh; lots of rosehips on the bushes here, ideal for making rosehip syrup:

Rosehips at North Warren   *Photo:* Rob Macklin

Rosehip Syrup
For 3-4 bottles
2lb rosehips
4.5 pints water
1lb sugar

"Remove stalks and mince or chop rosehips. Boil 3 pints of water then add rosehips, bring back to the boil, remove from the heat and leave to infuse for 15 minutes. Ladle rosehips and liquid through a scalded jelly bag or muslin and allow the bulk of the juice to drip through. Return the remaining pulp to the pan and add remaining 1.5 pints of boiling water. Re-boil, infuse again for 10 minutes and strain as before. Pour the juice into a clean pan and simmer until it measures approx. 1.5 pints. Add the sugar, stir to dissolve then boil for 5 minutes. Pour the syrup, while still hot, into warm, clean bottles within one inch of the top. Push in new corks (previously boiled for 15 minutes) not too tightly and tie with string. Place the bottles in a deep saucepan, on a false bottom, and fill with cold water to the level of the syrup. Bring slowly to the boil, simmer for five minutes to sterilize then remove from the pan. Remove string and press the corks firmly in. Dry the bottles and when corks are dry dip into melted paraffin wax to keep them air tight. Nice on its own it also makes a superb sauce for ice-cream."

Still lots of late summer flowers on the marshes, particularly yarrow, red clover and lady's bedstraw. Sea campion and the delightful, tightly packed orange and yellow snapdragons of common toadflax were in flower all over the beach.

Toadflax in flower on the beach   *Photo:* Rob Macklin

18th

An overcast and grey morning with brisk, squally showers – perfect for migration. At least 67 swallows and 32 house martins were battling south across the marshes. Meadow pipits moved through at a rate of 240 per hour and eight yellow wagtails picked off insects disturbed by the cattle. A flock of 90 goldfinches feeding on thistles brought a burst of colour to a grey day!

185

Yellow wagtail   *Photo:* Stuart Elsom

19th

An osprey caused a flurry of excitement over North Warren and Thorpe Meare. It caught two fish on the meare and another in the reedbed before flying up into a dead tree on the edge of the reedbed to feed. Many birds from Scotland and Scandinavia take time out to feed on the lakes and estuaries on the east coast before continuing their journey to their winter quarters in West Africa.

An osprey caused a
flurry of excitement
Photo: Stuart Elsom

September 20th

Sunny and warm with a light breeze so an ideal time to visit Havergate Island, near Orford. Large numbers of wigeon and teal, interspersed with occasional shelduck and pintail, were feeding on the saline lagoons. Several hundred avocets were roosting at high tide, providing a spectacular show as they made several short, wheeling flights. Redshanks were particularly abundant while there were a few grey plovers and a flock of 71 golden plovers, including one still in full summer plumage. Several little egrets were feeding in the shallows and these were joined by four exotic spoonbills which have become a regular summer feature on the island. Spoonbills feed by sweeping their bills through the shallow water, hoovering up the immense number of invertebrates found here. Walking up to the north end of the island I flushed a stunning short-eared owl.

The "pagodas" of Orfordness behind the lagoons at Havergate   *Photo:* Rob Macklin
Inset, spoonbills   *Photo:* Richard Thomas

An abundance of sea campion and a few sea pinks were still in flower on the shingle ridge. Masses of sea beet and sea wormwood were evident along the edges of the island and some of the lagoons were ablaze with the colour of autumnal, purple salicornia.

Sea pink on Havergate Island   *Photo:* Rob Macklin

October

> *October was named from the Latin word "Octo"*
> *being the eighth month in the Roman calendar.*
> *The Anglo-Saxons called it "Wyn Monath"*
> *as it was the season of wine-making.*
>
> *As part of the seasonal calendar, October*
> *is the time of the "Blood Moon" according*
> *to pagan beliefs.*

1st

A strong southerly wind is continuing to keep conditions mild; long sunny periods today with heavy showers from mid-afternoon. A young woodpigeon (a "squab") had fallen from a nest at River Hundred; two magpies soon found it and made off with it!

Honeysuckle, brown knapweed and harebells are all in flower on the Walks. I found a single specimen of wild clary on the beach. Ivy has come into full flower, providing an autumnal nectar source for a range of insects including red admirals. A fresh comma was at River Hundred and a small white butterfly at Sluice Cottage.

Brown knapweed was in flower on the Walks   *Photo:* Rob Macklin

An osprey has been hanging around for several days and was again seen fishing over the reedbed. Two late swallows flew south.

Purple sloes were dripping from the trees along the old railway track. The sloe or blackthorn is the ancestor of our cultivated plums and man has been eating it for thousands of years. The sloe makes such a good wine that, according to Brook, 200 years ago it was much used "by fraudulent wine merchants in adulterating port wine, for which purpose it is well adapted on account of its astringency, slight acidity and deep red colour".

Sloe gin is now a very popular drink and is traditionally made by gathering sloes in late September or October, pricking them with a skewer, half filling a bottle with them, adding a few spoonfuls of sugar and covering with gin. The purple, almond-flavoured liqueur is ready to drink by Christmas but improves with age. When the liquid is finished the sloes can be eaten, neat or processed. The pitted gin-soaked sloes can be dipped into melted chocolate which is then allowed to set.

As one countrywoman reported – "My uncle had a saying, 'I like my women fast and my gin sloe'."

Ripening sloes on the
old railway track
Photo: **Rob Macklin**

October

4th

St Francis Day. On this day swallows were thought to fly to the bottom of ponds to hibernate through the winter. The fact that swallows skim the surface of ponds and waterbodies for insects probably contributed to this particular folklore which persisted until Gilbert White's observations in the 18th Century in the "Natural History of Selborne".

Still sunny and unseasonably warm at 17°C with a southerly breeze. Several red admirals still on the wing plus occasional common darters and migrant hawker dragonflies. Masses of bright-orange rose-hips grace the bushes on North Marsh. Fresh white campion now in flower along the old railway track plus a late-flowering white rose.

Late-flowering white rose   *Photo:* Rob Macklin

6th

A very wet day with torrential rain, particularly in the early afternoon. Sunny later but breezy. Wigeon numbers have risen to 130 on the marshes and 51 resplendent lapwings were dotted across the fields. A female pintail was on South Marsh and two house martins were over the beach.

8th

Still fairly warm and sunny with a light south-westerly breeze. A marsh tit was calling agitatedly along the old railway track by the Three Arches bridge; a small group of long-tailed tits moved through the alders and willows calling constantly.

Still hordes of berries on the hawthorn bushes but just the odd blackbird taking advantage of the bounty – the main arrival of winter thrushes should make short work of them! The first of these, a redwing, flew in off the sea at Thorpe Common.

195

Hawthorn berries will provide a winter feast for thrushes   *Photo:* Rob Macklin

Saw a bittern flying languidly over the west end of Thorpe Meare and still 60 mute swans there. Three late small white butterflies were out along the field edges at Home Farm, Sizewell.

9th

Unseasonal temperatures of 20°C continue the Indian summer! A large female sparrowhawk flashed across the garden at River Hundred scattering the small birds around the feeders. The high tide wader roost on the beach held 90 ringed plovers and three dunlin.

October
10th

Walked through the south side of Dunwich Forest on a calm, dull day. Very few birds around although both green and great-spotted woodpeckers were active and six swallows were taking insects over an open area within the forest. Underneath the massed ranks of conifers and along the path edges bell heather is thriving and is still in flower, its purple blooms brightening up the darkness under the pines.

Bell heather in flower under pines in Dunwich Forest   *Photo:* Rob Macklin

More ancient Scots pines have escaped the harvester within the wood and mature oaks still survive on the outskirts. An unmanaged arable field by Rookyard Wood hosted flowering white campion, toadflax and common cat's-ear. On the bare ground both field pansy and corn spurrey were doing extremely well. I came across a "dinner-plate" sized parasol mushroom!

**Field pansy by
Rookyard Wood**
Photo: **Rob Macklin**

At Potton Hall flowering wild hops tumbled over ripe damsons in the hedgerows. The holly trees are full of berries here. Jays called incessantly from deep within the forest.

Wild hops were in flower at Potton Hall   *Photo:* Rob Macklin

198

October

12th

Wild geese do not usually arrive on the Suffolk coast until deep into mid-winter so I was very surprised to find a party of 10 white-fronted geese on North Marsh. Five grey herons were hunting for fish and amphibians along the dyke edges and a flock of 230 wigeon were tucking in to the plentiful grass.

Migrants have begun to arrive on the coast with a "fall" of song thrushes at Ness House and Thorpe Cliff, plus two much rarer yellow-browed warblers – striking, temporary visitors from northern Russia!

13th

A dawn visit to Thorpe Cliff for another look at the yellow-browed warbler was rewarded by just a fleeting glimpse before it moved off into the dense hawthorn scrub. The bird was located by its call and was moving through the sycamore trees. Large numbers of chaffinches had arrived accompanied by several bramblings, easily identified by their white rumps!

Male brambling   *Photo:* Stuart Elsom

Another superb, sunny day to 19°C with light easterly winds. A passing helicopter put up over 1,000 wildfowl on the marshes, including eight white-fronted geese.

Still a few butterflies on the wing, particularly red admirals but also a few small whites, small coppers and painted ladies; the latter were nectaring on sea aster at the Haven along with scores of honey bees and a silver Y moth.

Sea aster in flower at the Haven   *Photo:* Rob Macklin

16th

A rare visitor, a red-flanked bluetail, at Thorpe Common   *Photo:* Stuart Elsom

After yesterday's strong easterly winds it seemed distinctly possible that more migrants would turn up but I was not expecting such a rare visitor. Just after dawn an immature red-flanked bluetail was discovered in the bushes at Thorpe Common! I managed to re-locate the bird a little later and could clearly see the diagnostic white patch on the throat and the bluish tail. Small groups of redwings and song thrushes had also arrived.

October

On the beach 100 greenfinches were searching for any available seeds and were being shadowed by two kestrels, waiting for an opportunity to strike the unwary. A large amount of shingle has been deposited on the Ness, forming a steep cliff!

21st

Went up to Thorpe Common again to have another look at the bluetail! The bird was moving about unconcernedly through the bushes, seemingly unhindered by the large numbers of birdwatchers! Several hundred have been to see the bird over the past few days. A male blackcap was also here, feeding up on ripe blackberries. Most of "our" blackcaps leave these shores for southern Europe and Africa in the autumn, being replaced by their cousins from central Europe.

In the late afternoon three marsh harriers, including an immature male, were quartering the reedbed. Two swallows flew over. Still several red admirals on the wing.

Several red
admirals were
still on the wing
at River Hundred
Photo: Rob Macklin

October

Yews line the path to the war memorial   *Photo:* Rob Macklin

The yew trees at Aldringham Church are laden with berries which will provide a feast for winter thrushes, as well as our resident blackbirds.

Many plants are taking advantage of the extended warm weather, particularly red and white campion, bramble, nipplewort, ragwort, honeysuckle and yarrow. The churchyard is full of relatively old yew trees including a trimmed line to the war memorial. Parasol mushrooms have invaded the churchyard!

Yew berries at
Aldringham Church
Photo: Rob Macklin

207

I walked past the old "Providence Baptist Chapel", quiet now but an excellent spot for warblers and nightingales in the spring. I came across a horde of fly agarics on the Walks, the red caps shining brightly under the birch and gorse branches. This is one of the easiest species to recognise in Suffolk and its properties have been well documented for centuries. The common name of fly agaric comes from the practice of breaking the cap into platefuls of milk, used since medieval times to stupefy flies. It is also a strong hallucinogen when the cap is dried and swallowed without chewing and still used to this day in some native communities!

On the way home I found a magnificent seven-foot-high great mullein bursting with yellow flowers. Several red deer burst out of Square Covert.

Fly agaric, one of the easiest species to identify   *Photo:* Rob Macklin

28th

We held a volunteer work party on the Walks as our contribution to the national "Make a Difference Day". Thirty volunteers and staff cleared a couple of hectares of birch and gorse scrub and enjoyed baked potatoes for lunch from the embers of a roaring fire!

The voluntary work party at Aldringham Walks enjoyed baked potatoes from the embers of a roaring fire

Photo: Rob Macklin

In the afternoon a marbled duck was found amongst hundreds of teal on north marsh. A southern European species, it seems likely that this one was an escape from a wildfowl collection!

The end of British Summer Time.

29th

Still several red admirals on the wing and I disturbed a silver Y moth in Church Wood. At River Hundred 14 woodpigeons were feeding voraciously on masses of fallen beech mast.

*November derives from the Roman word "novem"
meaning nine, as it was the ninth month of the
Roman calendar. The Anglo-Saxons called this month
"Wind Monath" as cold winds began to blow.
It was also called "Blod Monath" as the cattle were
slaughtered for winter food.*

*In the Celtic world Samhain, literally meaning
"summer's end", falls on November 1st and marks
one of the two great doorways of the Celtic year.
Samhain marked the beginning of a whole new cycle,
just as the Celtic day began at night.
With the rise of Christianity, Samhain was changed
to Hallowmas or All Saints Day.*

*The poet Sir Walter Scott wrote in 1808:
"November's sky is chill and drear,
November's leaf is red and sear (withered)."*

1st

Strong north-westerly winds overnight have brought havoc to this part of the Suffolk coast with many low-lying areas flooded by salt water after a tremendous North Sea surge. North Warren escaped relatively lightly with just a foot of water on the road by Haven House at Thorpeness, following the old course of the Hundred river.

Further up the coast a 1,500-metre stretch of shingle ridge at Dingle Marshes has been completely washed away causing widespread saltwater incursion into the reedbeds at Westwood Marshes. Dingle Marshes themselves lie under several feet of salt water and Point Marsh suffered a huge fish-kill with hundreds of rudd lying dead on the surface. The dune frontage at Minsmere also suffered enormous damage although the secondary defence bank largely held, just a little over-topping! The whole of Blythburgh marshes up as far as Blyford bridge were under water and the main A12 road was closed all day.

The shape of things to come?

Dingle Marshes under salt water   *Photo:* Mike Page

3rd

With the advent of colder, northerly winds wildfowl numbers on the marshes are beginning to rise. Teal and wigeon numbers reached one thousand each and they were joined by small groups of shoveler and the ever-attractive pintails. Now that the boats have been withdrawn from

211

Thorpe Meare for the winter, the west end of this man-made lake has begun to attract more wildfowl with 60 gadwall and three little grebes joined by assorted mallards and moorhens.

Groups of starlings, some a hundred strong, were flying in off the sea and scores of blackbirds populated the bushes around the marshes, all visitors from northern Europe and Scandinavia.

Many of the local plants are still in flower including white and red campion, ragwort, yarrow, brown knapweed, bramble, white deadnettle, nipplewort, red clover, creeping thistle and redshank. Dogwood is not a common plant in this area, being more suited to calcareous soils; it was probably introduced at North Warren when the railway was constructed in the early part of the last century. However, some flowers are now blooming again!

Yarrow in autumn bloom   *Photo:* Rob Macklin

An extremely faded speckled wood butterfly on the old railway track was joined by several fresher-looking red admirals plus several ruddy and common darter dragonflies.

The now-dilapidated Sluice Cottage between Aldeburgh and Thorpeness

Photo:
Rob Macklin

Sluice Cottage has become a derelict ruin inhabited by breeding jackdaws, stock doves and blue tits. Thick bullace and bramble scrub surrounding the building is a haven for migrant birds. It is not that long ago that this building was inhabited by a marshman who would look after the livestock on the marshes and keep the sluices and dykes clear. There were never any facilities and even the water had to be carried in by hand from the Wentworth Hotel in Aldeburgh!

5th

Went up to Snape Warren where the birches and particularly the oaks, were still in full leaf. I came across a venerable, dying oak on the open heath; its stark branches providing superb perches for birds of prey. A very large, impenetrable holly tree stood nearby. Memories of spring were re-kindled by several woodlarks in full song, hanging in the air – a delightful, uplifting sound! I then put up two more pairs from the heavily rabbit-grazed grassland – the white eye-stripes and short tails very obvious.

Two jays flew away through the birches, screeching as they went and showing off their white rumps to good effect. Several patches of bell heather are still in flower!

The highest point of Snape Warren offers fantastic views across to Iken and west to the Maltings. A flock of 550 black-tailed godwits were being pushed off the mud by the incoming tide and they looked stunning as they flew straight over my head to their high-tide roost. Scores of shelduck and wigeon were out on the river and a few redshanks called as they slipped away. Hoary cress was still in flower on the edge of the saltmarsh where four rather drab-looking rock pipits searched for insects along the tide line.

Snape Maltings from the river
Photo:
Rob Macklin

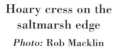

Hoary cress on the saltmarsh edge
Photo: Rob Macklin

November

9th

Sunny and relatively mild, still no sign of any frost. Two turnstones were feeding along the tide line on the beach, looking for food amongst the debris. A further 24 birds were on the beach at Slaughden.

Turnstone at Aldeburgh   *Photo:* Stuart Elsom

10th

The first frost of the winter! Small flocks of linnets and skylarks were on maize stubble at Abbey Farm in Snape. In the hedgerows 60 chaffinches were intent on avoiding the attentions of two marauding sparrowhawks. A mistle thrush was singing at River Hundred.

12th

Went up to the Walks for a look at the new reservoir behind Square Covert. Although only half full it is providing a real attraction for diving ducks boasting 32 tufted ducks, a female pochard and goldeneye but most surprisingly of all a female long-tailed duck, a very scarce species in Suffolk which is usually found on the open sea.

Long-tailed ducks are scare visitors to Suffolk   *Photo:* Stuart Elsom

A stunning male stonechat was perched up on the crest of a clump of gorse while three Dartford warblers were much more difficult to see as they flitted through the heather.

13th

Paid a visit to the relatively new Suffolk Wildlife Trust reserve at Church Farm, Thorington, near Blythburgh. The wood was a colourful array of autumn colours with the field maples a glorious bright yellow.

Field maple
hedge at
Thorington
in glorious
autumn
colour
Photo:
Rob Macklin

Spindle trees at
Church Farm
looked very dapper,
sporting bright
coral-pink berries
Photo: Rob Macklin

The spindle trees looked very dapper, sporting bright coral-pink berries.
A fine stand of alders bordered the wetland areas of the farm.

The impressive church of St. Peter sports a round tower which has been
variously described as mid-Saxon, late-Saxon, Saxo-Norman and Norman! There
are many round-towered churches in East Anglia and perhaps the most obvious
reason for their presence is the lack of local stone.

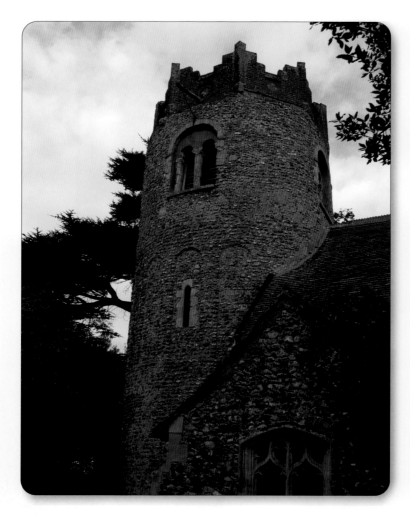

The Church of St. Peter at Thorington   *Photo:* Rob Macklin

The fabric of East Anglian churches is a mixture of flint and rubble, with costly stone imported from elsewhere to mould doorways, windows, quoins and parapets. Odd pieces of stone waste were cut into shapes which framed whole or knapweed flints to produce the famous East Anglian flushwork. Where a Suffolk church presents a solid stone exterior, the building usually has a rubble filling! The churchyard is full of lime and yew trees, a haven for tawny owls and collared doves. A female sparrowhawk flashed overhead evading the unwelcome attention of a carrion crow.

November
17th

S unny and mild, although a strong southerly wind. A female marsh harrier drifted low over the swaying reeds while a female kestrel hovered intently over the thick vegetation on the banks of the reedbed. Broad-buckler fern was growing out of a wound on a riverside alder tree.

Broad-buckler fern growing out of a riverside alder
Photo: Rob Macklin

Sycamores and sweet chestnuts are now a vivid yellow, the birches and willows are turning but the oaks and alders remain steadfastly green!

Bright yellow sycamores and sweet chestnuts at North Warren
Photo: Rob Macklin

November

18th

Walked along the shingle ridge from Dunwich towards Walberswick; most of Dingle Marshes were under sea-water after the latest breach of the shingle ridge. There is now a huge gap out to the sea and no viable way to repair it. Small numbers of ducks were enjoying the flooded conditions including mallard, shoveler, gadwall, teal and wigeon plus over 200 greylag geese.

A grey heron took flight from the reeds and a little egret sailed elegantly past. Sea campion and toadflax were still in flower on the landward side of the ridge, having escaped the worst ravages of the incoming tide.

Dingle Marshes after a breach of the shingle ridge   *Photo:* Rob Macklin

19th

A light frost preceded a bright and sunny winter's day. Numbers of wildfowl are beginning to increase on the marshes, notably 1,400 wigeon, 860 teal and 29 superb-looking pintail.

Wigeon and dunlin at North Warren   *Photo:* Richard Thomas

The flocks of Canada and greylag geese have been joined by 90 barnacle geese
and a red-breasted goose; the latter has been on the Suffolk coast for the past few
years and has probably escaped from a wildfowl collection. A high tide at
Slaughden has brought 170 dunlin, 54 ringed plovers and over 200 lapwings onto
the marshes.

Several Cetti's warblers were tempted into song and a bittern flew sedately
over the reedbed. A dog otter was searching for fish and eels at the back of
Thorpe Meare and I watched him twisting and turning through the waters,
seemingly oblivious to my presence.

25th

A wild, wet and stormy November day but still exceptionally mild. Autumn
has finally arrived with most of the trees, particularly the beeches,
metamorphosing into their golden autumn colours.

Golden beech tree at River Hundred   *Photo:* Rob Macklin

26th

Walked up through Mumbery Hills, a little-known area on the west edge of Minsmere. I had taken no more than a few paces along the track when a young "two-pointer" stag bolted out of the gorse bushes right in front of me and away through the trees. I came across a large, old crag pit where a rowan tree was perched perilously on the lip.

Three Konik ponies (of Polish origin) were grazing on the edge of Meadow Marsh, effectively creating open areas within the fen, the very reason why they were introduced to the reserve.

Konik ponies at Minsmere, carrying out important conservation management work
Photo: Rob Macklin

Generally quiet in the birch woods, a mixed tit flock including long-tailed and marsh tits moving through the trees and the plaintive call of a bullfinch in the background. One particular area of the wood was dominated by mature oak trees with a thick under-storey of hollies – possibly indicating an area of semi-ancient woodland.

Long-tailed tit
amongst the birches
Photo: Stuart Elsom

A mixed herd of red deer, including several stags, bolted out of a clearing and away through the woods. The open clearing reeked of the pungent scent of the deer lending a primeval feel to the moment. A jay flew across the clearing carrying acorns to bury for another day.

A group of burnished copper larch trees shone brightly in the morning light. A heavy peal of thunder preceded a fierce thunderstorm and a spectacular rainbow formed over Minsmere. A carrion crow and a sparrowhawk sparred intermittently over the wood before fleeing the coming storm.

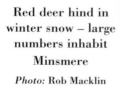

Red deer hind in winter snow – large numbers inhabit Minsmere

Photo: Rob Macklin

**Storm over
Minsmere**
Photo: Rob Macklin

27th

S unny, breezy and still extremely mild with both common darter dragonflies
and red admirals on the wing. I walked up over the Walks this afternoon
coming across a small mixed tit flock in Church Wood; a treecreeper
searched for insects on the scaly bark of a Corsican pine. A male green
woodpecker, clearly showing his red moustachial stripe, probed the grassland
for insects and was off in a flash of his yellow rump as I approached!

**Treecreeper
hunting for insects**
Photo: Stuart Elsom

November

Although it is late November the unusually mild weather has encouraged many plants to continue flowering, particularly red and white campion, common fiddleneck, bugloss, smooth sow-thistle, groundsel, cut-leaved cranesbill, scentless mayweed and woody nightshade.

29th

A light ground frost but sunny and warm all day with a light westerly breeze. Walked across Westleton Heath to Dunwich through the site of the old Westleton sawmill, long since defunct but a reminder of busier times. A male kestrel showed off his bluish head and tail which shone in the sunlight as he hunted around the crag pit. A natterjack toad pond has been constructed here and several common darters were making good use of the shallow waters.

Kestrel   *Photo:* Mark Breaks

Above, a winter view across
Westleton Heath, and right, a new pond
created at Mount Pleasant

Photo: Rob Macklin

The gorse was still flowering well and its coconut scent filled the air. A low buzz from deep within the heather announced the presence of a Dartford warbler which quickly disappeared into the cover afforded by the gorse. The open heath is quiet in mid-winter!

I skirted around the edge of Grimston's Covert passing more excavated pools, catching the calls of marsh tits from the pine woods. Approaching Dunwich Heath I could hear two woodlarks in full song from high up in the sky – so evocative of spring. On through Greyfriars Wood, admiring the prolific clumps of male fern in the dappled sunlight.

In Dunwich village the house sparrows seemed quite abundant and very confiding. After a good ploughman's lunch at the Ship Inn I continued through the south edge of Dunwich Forest and out on to Westleton Heath. A bright male Dartford warbler was looking for insects around the base of the birch scrub and a male stonechat perched atop a gorse bush in the late afternoon sun.

November
30th

Muntjac deer have colonised the Suffolk coast in recent years and, unlike other deer, are fairly tolerant of humans. The gardens at River Hundred usually host several animals and today a youngster was trying out his butting skills on his father, who walked off in disgust – then his mother, who seemed resigned to her fate!

A female kestrel was perched up overlooking the heath and scanning the ground for potential prey while 50-odd rooks and jackdaws were probing the short turf on the acid grassland for leatherjackets and other insects. In contrast, 19 curlews were picking food off the surface of the ground with their much finer bills.

Our Manx Loghtan sheep are now grazing one area of the heath while the Wiltshire Horns have moved from the Walks to another area on the Warren. Grass growth has been phenomenal in such a mild and wet autumn so there should be no shortage of food for many weeks to come!

**Wiltshire Horns at
North Warren**

Photo: Rob Macklin

The spectacular barnacle goose flock on North Marsh held 104 birds together with the expected red-breasted goose while lapwings are up to 700. A far corner of North Marsh turned up a small flock of "wild" white-fronted geese. A splendid deep-red male bullfinch perched up proudly on a hawthorn bush and a recently ploughed field backing on to the reserve had attracted 150 linnets and a few chaffinches.

December

December used to be the tenth month of the Roman year, hence the name from the Latin "decem".

The Anglo-Saxons called December "Yule Monath" derived from the custom of burning the yule log at this time. In the northern hemisphere December is said to mark the beginning of winter and is purported to bring rain, wind and snow.

1st

O vercast, grey and dull with occasional showers but still extremely mild. A veteran hawthorn tree at River Hundred is absolutely covered in a pale grey lichen *Cladonia sp.*

Cladonia lichen on veteran hawthorn   *Photo:* Rob Macklin

229

Pheasants at River Hundred   *Photo:* Rob Macklin

Feeding the birds in the morning now involves being ambushed by seven pheasants, including two males, who have come to expect their daily rations.

High tides at Slaughden have brought 200 black-tailed godwits, 200 dunlin and several hundred lapwings onto a roost on South Marsh.

6th

A welcome lull after several wet and stormy days, sunny, mild and breezy. Went over to Abbey Farm at Snape this afternoon. Several hundred woodpigeons were feeding on maize stubble and over a thousand rooks and jackdaws joined the feast. Meanwhile, 230 lapwings were enjoying the flooded splashes on the adjoining marshes towards Langham Bridge.

Several "arable weeds" are still in flower, particularly scentless mayweed, pineapple weed, groundsel, field speedwell, dandelion and nipplewort.

A dearth of smaller birds – just a few chaffinches and yellowhammers in the hedgerows.

December
7th

One extreme to the other, from sunny and mild to torrential rain and storm-force winds from the south-west. Suffolk in its unpredictable glory!

South of Walberswick village the sea was crashing into the shingle ridge threatening to overtop it once again! Six marsh harriers were in the air together over Westwood Marsh and a little egret feeding in the shallows lent the day a "Mediterranean" feel.

Little egret, a recent coloniser from Europe   *Photo:* Stuart Elsom

December
9th

The first real frost of the winter, everything white, crisp and cold! Our winter work party of nine hardy souls cleared invasive bramble and birch scrub from the open heath at Snape Warren. Some previously cleared areas have been colonised by a delightful light green lichen *"Cladonia digitata"*, identifiable by the masses of small trumpets.

Cladonia digitata on the heath   *Photo:* Rob Macklin

10th

Another hard frost, even more severe than the previous day, then sunny and cold – a perfect winter's day! Most of Thorpe Meare was frozen as well as the shallow, flooded areas on the marshes.

A superb array of geese on the grazing marshes included scattered flocks of 318 greylag and 211 Canada geese. The higher and drier Sluice Marsh had attracted 90 pied barnacle geese, 44 white-fronted geese and now two delightful red-breasted geese. A hunting marsh harrier scattered most of the ducks and waders but the geese remained supremely indifferent.

One of the two delightful red-breasted geese, with brent   *Photo:* Stuart Elsom

Numbers of the more unusual ducks are on the rise and include 64 shoveler, 134 gadwall and 50 splendid pintail. A wintering ruff has joined 31 black-tailed godwits on North Marsh and a water rail squealed from the dense cover of the reeds. Still lots of rosehips available.

11th

Torrential rain and storm-force winds abated by early afternoon. I took the opportunity to carry out another marsh harrier roost count at the main reedbed. The first birds arrived at 1455 hours but did not go down into the reeds until 1524 hours. Most of the harriers flew in high from the south, probably spending the daylight hours hunting over Orfordness and Sudbourne Marshes. The majority of the birds were females although two adult and two immature males made up the final tally of 22 birds.

A male marsh harrier coming in to roost   *Photo:* Stuart Elsom

As dusk deepened a ghostly apparition appeared over the reedbed banks, a barn owl out on an evening hunting foray. The owl was flecked brown on white upperparts and clear white under the wings and on the body. Barn owls will often hunt in the fading winter daylight as they become desperate for food to survive the long winter nights! Small flotillas of jackdaws flew over to their chosen roost and 70 carrion crows were extremely vocal as they settled down for the night.

Barn Owl: a ghostly figure   *Photo: Stuart Elsom*

Dusk over the reedbed at North Warren   *Photo:* Rob Macklin

The sky was on fire! *"Red Sky at Night – Shepherd's Delight, Red Sky in the Morning – Shepherd's Warning"*.

13th

Walked over Blaxhall Common this morning. A male merlin, our smallest falcon, flew strongly and directly across the heath, scattering foraging parties of meadow pipits. A great-spotted woodpecker flew over in typical bounding flight while several green woodpeckers and jays called from the nearby woods. One never thinks of jays as members of the crow family with their bright chestnut plumage, white rump and blue-flecked wings!

Hoar frost at River Hundred   *Photo:* Rob Macklin

23rd

S hingle Street is one of the most remote hamlets on the Suffolk coast and looked particularly bleak and desolate on a grey and cold winter's day. It is possible to see at least three Martello Towers from here, built by His Majesty's government of the day to see off the threat of Napoleonic invasion in the 19th Century.

The Martello Tower
at Shingle Street
Photo: Rob Macklin

Short-eared owl   *Photo:* Stuart Elsom

This is one of the best places in Suffolk to see short-eared owls in winter but, alas, today no sign of them although several hunting kestrels were searching for small mammals across the pastures. Small flocks of lapwings and starlings, plus five curlews, were feeding on the grass amongst the outwintering cattle. Two male stonechats continually dived into the grass from reedstems, presumably hunting for any available insects.

Later in the afternoon I went down through the silent birch woods to count the marsh harriers into roost, disturbing a woodcock along the way. A large brown rat scurried back into its burrow under a Scots pine. I waited at the reedbed until dark and watched 18 harriers come in, all from the south. It seems incredible that as recently as 1971 just one pair of marsh harriers were breeding in Britain, at Minsmere, and wintering birds were unknown, spending their winters in southern Europe and Africa. A full survey of the Suffolk coast last Sunday came up with over 100 birds roosting in our major reedbeds.

24th

Cold and grey with a brisk north-easterly wind and just a mere suspicion of blue sky. Thirty great black-backed gulls, our largest resident gull, stood out amongst their smaller cousins in the roost on the marshes.

Amongst the geese, 92 barnacles and two red-breasted geese remain. The truly wild populations of barnacle geese breed mainly on Arctic islands and coasts and only occasionally visit Suffolk in mid-winter. However, feral breeding birds have built up their numbers in Suffolk and on the coast of Holland; it is likely that these birds are represented in the current flock. Red-breasted geese winter in eastern Europe and rarely visit the UK and our two birds have almost certainly escaped from wildfowl collections. But they are stunning birds for all that!

Barnacle geese on the North Marsh
Photo: Rob Macklin

December
25th

Christmas Day! Dull, grey and mild. Robins are singing in the garden at River Hundred.

Robin in song on Christmas Day   *Photo:* Stuart Elsom

W alked up into Kenton and Goose Hills on the Sizewell Estate. The woods here are a mixture of planted Scots and Corsican pines, the latter a firm favourite of foresters as it grows generally straight and true, providing good-quality timber. I came across two lime trees which had been coppiced in the past but have now been allowed to grow towards maturity.

Mature coppiced lime trees at Sizewell   *Photo:* Rob Macklin

A wetter area of pools and rhines has been totally overwhelmed by *"Rhodedendron ponticum"*. A garden escapee, it has built up an impenetrable thicket here to the exclusion of almost any other species. A pair of marsh tits were feeding on alder seed in the tree tops while several coal tits preferred to forage amongst the pine cones on the neighbouring conifers.

Coal tit   *Photo:* Mark Breaks

A Holm oak, an evergreen species from the Mediterranean which has been widely planted and is quite capable of self-seeding, stood alone in the stark, bare wood. A few bramble flowers were still out along the sheltered woodland edge while plants such as alexanders, stinging nettles and ground ivy all retained green leaf vigour! I found a bright orange *"Cortinarius"* fungus growing on and amongst pine logs.

Cortinarius fungus
Photo: Rob Macklin

December
30th

Heavy rain overnight has brought the water levels right up on the marshes and I was forced to adjust the main sluice to allow superfluous water to drain off at low tide. More white-fronted geese have arrived from the Low Countries and at least 180 were grazing contentedly across North Marsh amongst the Canada, greylag and barnacle geese.

White-fronted geese on the North Marsh   *Photo:* Richard Thomas

Seven cormorants were resting on the dyke edges while 10 shelducks and at least 50 pintail brought a splash of colour to the marshes. Three pochards were diving for fish in the deeper dykes. Two sparrowhawks brought a touch of panic to proceedings, making several hundred lapwings and 136 black-tailed godwits very nervous.

Still exceptionally mild with temperatures up to 13°C persuading a mistle thrush into song at Fen Cottages. A small group of long-tailed tits in the birch trees along the old railway track were constantly contact-calling with each other while both treecreeper and wren uttered short bursts of song.

December
31st

The year ends on an exceptionally mild note with southerly winds, watery sunshine and light showers, a little like April. At River Hundred blue tits and coal tits have burst into song, goldcrests are calling amongst the pines while chaffinches and greenfinches vie for supremacy at the sunflower feeders.

The dry climate of the Suffolk coast does not provide ideal conditions for mosses and ferns but the walls of Aldeburgh Church support a thriving population of maindenhair spleenwort and wall rue. The conservation area within the churchyard hosts a superb ancient holly which was still holding on to a few berries. Moles have invaded the churchyard.

Left, maidenhair spleenwort
at Aldeburgh Church

Photo: Rob Macklin

Below, tundra bean geese over
North Warren,
a true winter scene

Photo: Steve Valentine